Paul The Pastor

GOD'S WORD TODAY VII

A New Study Guide to the Bible

Emil A. Wcela

Paul The Pastor

2 2 7
Wec

His Teaching
in the First Letter to the Corinthians

Suggestions for Reflection
by Sr. Jeanne Monahan O.P.

PUEBLO PUBLISHING COMPANY

NEW YORK

13947

Nihil Obstat: Daniel V. Flynn, J.C.D.
                Censor Librorum

Imprimatur: ✠ James P. Mahoney, D.D.
              Vicar General,
              Archdiocese of New York
              August 26, 1975

Design: Frank Kacmarcik, D.F.A.

The text of The New American Bible, Copyright © 1970
by the Confraternity of Christian Doctrine, Washington,
D.C. (Books 1 Samuel to 2 Maccabees, 1969) is reproduced
herein by license of said Confraternity of Christian Doctrine.
All rights reserved.

Copyright © 1976 Pueblo Publishing Company, Inc.,
1860 Broadway, New York, N.Y. 10023
All rights reserved.

ISBN: 0-916134-26-1

Printed in the United States of America

CONTENTS

PREFACE

Interest in the Scriptures continues to grow. Men and women individually and in groups read, reflect on, discuss, pray from the Bible. I have taught, led, participated in such groups. This participation has convinced me that, despite all the worthwhile material on the Bible already available, there are still gaps to be filled for those people who truly care about the Bible but have had little or no preparation to extract its riches.

Several excellent guides to the Bible exist in the format of booklet series in which each volume provides commentary and explanation on a separate book of the Bible. However, for someone becoming acquainted with the Bible, to work through each book one by one can be a formidable task.

Other books focus on themes and main ideas distilled from the whole Bible. As valuable as such theologies and over-all views are, there is still a need for a familiarity with the *text* of the Bible itself.

In this series, substantial portions of the Scriptures — extensive enough to convey style, language, tone — are the indispensable starting point. Essential background and explanation are provided and the lasting import of the text is suggested. Possibilities for individual or group reflection are offered.

When the reader has completed this series, he will have encountered many themes and main ideas, and this through a selected and guided reading of the text itself. This over-all view can be filled in by further study of the individual books of the Bible.

The general plan emerges from a listing of the titles in this series. It is my strong recommendation that anyone using the series begin with Volume I. If the principles presented there are grasped, the spadework will be done for understanding what follows.

Vol. I: THE BIBLE: What it is and how it developed.

Vol. II: BASIC BELIEFS IN GENESIS AND EXODUS

Vol. III: THE PROPHETS: God's spokesmen through the years.

Vol. IV: THE STORY OF ISRAEL: God's people through the years.

Vol. V: JESUS, HIS WORD AND WORK: The gospels of Matthew, Mark and Luke.

Vol. VI: THE GOSPEL OF JOHN.

Vol. VII: PAUL THE PASTOR: His teaching in the First Letter to the Corinthians.

Vol. VIII: PAUL THE THEOLOGIAN: His teaching in the Letter to the Romans.

"Indeed, God's word is living and effective, sharper than any two-edged sword. It penetrates and divides soul and spirit, joints and marrow; it judges the reflections and thoughts of the heart" (Hebrews 4:12).

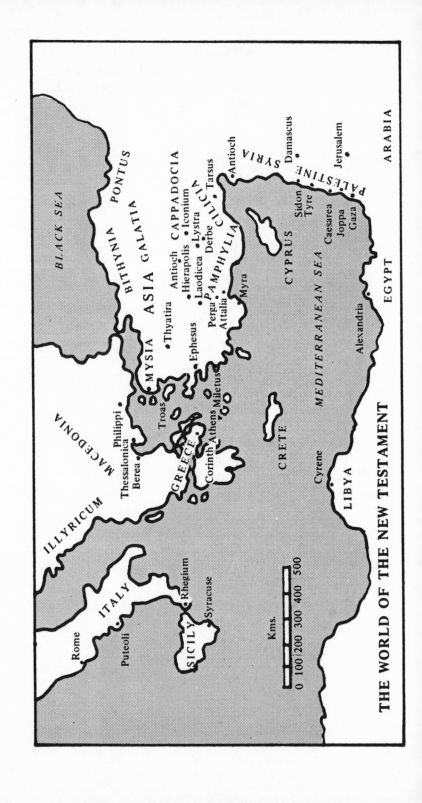

THE WORLD OF THE NEW TESTAMENT

CHAPTER I

ABOUT PAUL AND LETTERS

HOW PAUL COMMUNICATED – LETTERS

Paul's message has reached us in the form of letters.

Did you ever rummage through the attic or wherever it is
that memorabilia of your family are kept? I have, and
found letters and post cards 50, 60, 70 years old. Most of
them are from people I didn't know to my grandparents and
great-grandparents. They talk about people I never met, situations I never lived through, places I never visited. Many are
written in a foreign language with which I am only passingly
familiar.

I can fill in some of the background. For example, when one
young man wrote from England in 1916, I know he had fled
there as a refugee from the war raging through his homeland.

Another post card is marked, "From Venice" and also bears
a date during the First World War. From other information
I know the picture of canals was not the souvenir of a plea-
sure trip but a link with home for a homesick young sailor
who stopped at Venice during his tour of duty with the
United States Navy.

So it could go on. I could spend hours reading those cards
and letters written many years ago. And how unreal it would
be for me to believe that simply through the words, I could
appreciate all the emotion and life and experience expressed.

Problems are inevitable because of a number of character-istics of personal letters.

LETTERS ARE A SUBSTITUTE FOR A FACE-TO-FACE MEETING

Letters do not permit the leisure to say all that we might like. There's not the time, the space, to communicate to the one to whom we're writing all that's on our minds. And our hands soon get tired of writing. Five or six handwritten or even typed pages is a long letter. Yet those pages that took so long to write can be read in ten minutes.

If we were meeting someone we hadn't seen for a long time, ten minutes would hardly be time to say, "It's good to see you again."

Obviously, then, letters are going to be rather economical in what they say and how they say it. They leave a lot for the intended reader to fill in from past experience, from previous contacts between the two persons corresponding, and so on. And this presumed background will remain a mystery to the third party who reads the letter unless he has some way of reconstructing it.

LETTERS PINPOINT SPECIAL MOMENTS

Generally letters speak about very specific and personal situations of the correspondents. A letter carries to a friend the news that Uncle Fred has died. A response is dashed off by the friend expressing sympathy. How often we our-selves have written, or read in a letter, "I was sorry to hear about Uncle Fred," or "Too bad about your neighbor," or "I hope your son is feeling better." And that's all.

The letter does not explain what happened to Uncle Fred, or the neighbor, or the son. That information came by way of another letter or phone call or conversation. To put the whole jigsaw puzzle together, you have to know about the other letter or phone call or conversation.

How many references like these I found in that old family correspondence in the attic! They will remain forever a mystery because they are the life material of other people living in another age.

LETTERS ARE WRITTEN IN THE STYLE OF THEIR TIME AND REFLECT WHAT WAS HAPPENING THEN

Not only is the personal history of the writer reflected in his letters but also the history of his time.

Can you imagine what it will be like for someone who, a thousand years from now, finds a collection of personal letters from the 1970's and comes across "Watergate," "streaking," "rock and roll," "Palestine guerillas," "cook-out," "folk Mass."

If he wants a real grasp of the letters, he will do his best to study the history of the times to find out all the hidden meanings these words carried.

A map of Washington may show Watergate as a building complex. It cannot inform about the tragic scandal attached to these apartments and the crisis that faced the American presidency and caused the resignation of a president.

The curious reader in the 2970's could look up an ancient English dictionary from the 1970's and discover that "to streak" means "to form streaks or stripes in or on; to stripe." This will leave him as unaware as he was before of the peculiar activity that this word designated in the middle 1970's.

He may put "folk" and "Mass" together and conjecture that this was some kind of liturgy for people. But who else is the liturgy for? Literal definitions of words alone will fail to convey the significance of the phenomenon of the "folk Mass" in the 1970's.

It should be fairly clear that, whether a letter-writer intends it or not, his letters are going to be filled with all manner of references to what is going on around him. These references will carry no explanations, no definitions. They will be taken for granted, the presumption being that the one reading the letter will understand the references since they are part of his daily life too.

A thousand years later is another story. The life, the customs, the news, that pulsed through the letters originally will be long dead. How then will that reader, far off in the future, wipe the dust of the ages from people, places, events, that made the letters throb with life?

The only way to know intimately the letter and the letter-writer is to study carefully the circumstances and the times in which the letter was born.

PAUL AS A LETTER WRITER

Paul wrote letters just as anyone else does. True, his letters are part of God's message, but they are written in the words of a man. This man lived through a lifetime of vivid experiences. The letters he has left distill part of this experience.

Like all letters, Paul's are a substitute for a face-to-face encounter. We cannot expect to find in their necessarily limited content all that Paul ever taught or said or experienced.

Like all letters, Paul's are situational. They talk to specific situations or problems and leave unsaid or unwritten whole areas of his life and thought. Some parts of his letters are written in answer to letters sent to him or to messages carried to him by word of mouth. These letters and messages are now lost.

Like all letters, Paul's reflect the style and history of the time when they were written. They are filled with the events and people that were the topics of conversation then. Paul wrote in the Greek and in the letter form popular in his day. Just notice all the brief, unexplained personal references in

4

the Letter to the Romans, chapter 16. "I commend to you our sister Phoebe, who is a deaconess of the church of Cenchrae . . .she has been of help to many, including myself. Give my greetings to Prisca and Aquila; they were my fellow workers in the service of Christ Jesus and even risked their lives for the sake of mine. Remember me also to the congregation that meets in their house . . .My greetings to Mary, who has worked hard for you, and to Andronicus and Junias, my kinsmen and fellow prisoners . . .Greetings to Rufus, a chosen servant of the Lord, and to his mother, who has been a mother to me as well."

Who were all these people? What was their connection with Paul? What was their place in the Christian community? From these few lines themselves we will never know.

To believe that all the weight of what Paul wished to communicate can be gotten by a simple reading of the text is an over-simplification. That would require a miracle of communication between God and each person who reads Paul's letters today. The Scriptures do not show us that kind of God, a God who, in some supernatural way, gives each reader the background information he needs. God reveals himself through the talents and hard work of men he chooses. And it is through our talents and hard work that we must try to probe the word of God in the letters of Paul to discover what God is saying to us today.

PAUL'S LIFE BEFORE HIS CONVERSION

Paul was born some time in the years that we would calculate as 1 to 10 A. D. In Jewish circles, he went by a name famous in Israelite history, Saul. To non-Jewish associates, he was known as Paul.

The city of Tarsus is in the region of Asia Minor known as Cilicia. Today, the area is part of southeastern Turkey. Tarsus, not much to look at in our day, was noteworthy in Paul's time. Situated at the mouth of a river where the foothills of the Taurus mountains began to thrust up, it bustled with trade and commerce. Its port and roads fed in a constant stream of trade. It enjoyed a reputation for the number and quality of its schools and was recognized as a center of culture.

Here Paul was born. His parents were devout Jews and their son was reared as a pious observer of the ancient faith. At the same time, living in the kind of bustling, cosmopolitan city that Tarsus was, Paul also came into contact with Greek and other cultures flourishing around him.

According to Acts 22.3, Paul studied at Jerusalem under the famous rabbi, Gamaliel. Paul says of himself, "I made progress in Jewish observance far beyond most of my contemporaries, in my excess of zeal to live out all the traditions of my ancestors" (Gal 1.14). He belonged to the Pharisees, the most orthodox branch within the Judaism of his time. The Pharisees were rigorous in their concern for keeping the biblical laws which regulated all aspects of human conduct.

Paul never forgot his Jewishness. In the heat of a later controversy, he wrote about some who were belittling him, "Are they Hebrews? So am I! Are they Israelites? So am I! Are they the seed of Abraham? So am I!" (2 Cor 11. 22).

Paul's zeal for Judaism was enough of a force in his life to drive him to hostile pursuit of the followers of Jesus. "You know that I went to extremes in persecuting the church of God and tried to destroy it" (Gal 1.13).

PAUL'S CONVERSION

About the year 36, a startling change took place in Paul.

A description of the experience that caused it is found in three passages in the Acts of the Apostles, 9.3—19; 22.6—16; 26.12—18. Here is the familiar story of the persecutor on his way to ferret out Christians in the city of Damascus. A blinding light; the heavenly voice, "Saul, Saul, why do you persecute me?"; blindness; baptism in Damascus.

Paul in his letters gives no details about the conversion experience except to stress its results. "But the time came when he who had set me apart before I was born and called me by his favor chose to reveal his Son to me, that I might spread among the Gentiles the good tidings concerning him" (Gal 1.15-16).

Paul himself and the accounts in Acts agree that his conversion was not something he was gradually moving toward by an increasingly sympathetic contact with Christianity. Paul's dramatic change was not from within. It was from beyond him, from God who touched him and changed the direction of his life.

Paul and the accounts in Acts also agree on what his conversion brought him to do. He was to become not only a believer, not only a preacher. Paul was to have as his special concern bringing the Good News about Jesus to the Gentiles, the non-Jewish world.

PAUL'S LIFE AFTER CONVERSION

The next decade of Paul's life is something of a mystery because very little information is provided by Paul himself or by anyone else. Some clues can be found in Galatians 1.17–24.

Paul says that, after his conversion, he went to "Arabia," probably modern Syria and Jordan. After a time he returned to the city of Damascus.

During these three years, Paul embarked on his new life's work of preaching Jesus. The results of that work are not preserved except in references like 2 Corinthians 11.32, where Paul relates that an official "was keeping a close watch on the city in order to arrest me, but I was lowered in a basket through a window in the wall and escaped his hands."

7

About the year 40, Paul had his first contact with the original band of Jesus' followers. He writes, "I went up to Jerusalem to get to know Cephas, with whom I stayed fifteen days. I did not meet any other apostles except James, the brother of the Lord" (Gal 1.18-19). What happened between Paul and Peter (Cephas) during this encounter, we are not told. There must have been agreement about Paul's mission to the Gentiles because after the meeting, he continued what he had been doing.

After the Jerusalem visit, Paul continued evangelizing in Syria and Cilicia.

THE MISSIONARY JOURNEYS

If we follow the narrative provided by Acts, Paul spent the years from about 46 to 58 in intensive missionary activity. This period is traditionally divided into three journeys.

First Journey: 46-49 A.D.; Cyprus and Turkey; Acts 13.3-14. 26 3-14. 26; returned to Antioch.
Second Journey: 49-52 A.D.; Turkey and Greece; Acts 15. 40-18. 22; returned to Jerusalem and Antioch.
Third Journey: 54-57 A.D.; Turkey and Greece; Acts 18. 23-21. 17; returned to Jerusalem.

Acts provides a version of the geographical and chronological details of these journeys and a sampling of incidents. It is sufficient here to note that Paul seems to have followed a standard procedure in the places he visited. He sought out the Jews and preached first to them. Generally he was not very successful in turning them toward Jesus as the Messiah and Lord. He then carried his message to the non-Jews. Here he met with more success, organizing communities of newly-converted Christians.

These bland words run the danger of disguising the adventures that filled his days and nights. Paul himself writes of what he encountered. "Five times at the hands of the Jews I received

forty lashes less one; three time I was beaten with rods; I
was stoned once, shipwrecked three times; I passed a day and
a night on the sea. I traveled continually, endangered by
floods, robbers, my own people, the Gentiles; imperiled in
the city, in the desert, at sea, by false brothers; enduring
labor, hardship, many sleepless nights; in hunger and thirst and
frequent fastings, in cold and nakedness" (2 Cor 11.24-27).

In some cities he remained for only a few weeks. In others,
he spent longer periods — a year and a half at Corinth, two to
three years at Ephesus.

AN EARLY CRISIS

A crucial issue was facing the Church during those early years.
The relationship between Judaism and Christianity had to
be made clear.

As long as the first Christians were all Jews who had accepted
Jesus, they might keep their traditional Jewish observances,
adding to them their new faith in God's work through Jesus.
However, once non-Jews began to accept the Gospel in some
numbers, the question had to be asked. "Must one accept
Judaism and its practices — such as circumcision — if one is
to be a Christian? " The issue, to put it another way, was
whether faith in Jesus and life according to that faith was
something new, unique, independent or a simple development
of Judaism.

An account of how the early Church attempted to face this
very fundamental theological issue is found in Acts 15. The
events related make up the so-called "Council of Jerusalem"
of the year 49 or 50. This gathering was an important event
for Paul and his special vocation. According to the narrative,
the leaders of the Church, including Peter and James, met
for discussion and decided that converts to Christianity who
were not of Jewish background need not keep to the Jewish
observances.

The details of this meeting are difficult to establish exactly to the satisfaction of scholars but there is no doubt that the young Church grappled with this question with far-reaching consequences. "Is salvation through Jesus alone, or through Jesus plus the Jewish law? "

The answer, loud and clear, was that faith in Jesus and that alone makes man what he should be before God.

This answer, however rendered or publicized, was an approval of Paul's manner of operating. He wrote, "Those who were the acknowledged pillars, James, Cephas, and John, gave Barnabas and me the handclasp of fellowship, signifying that we should go the Gentiles as they to the Jews" (Gal 2.9).

Christianity, with roots in the religion of Israel, would not simply be a sect of Judaism. It was unique, based on the unique work of God through Jesus. More and more would it stand outside of the love-hate relationship that the ancient world had with Judaism.

Judaism was admired because of the vigor with which it testified to its one God in the midst of the confusing gallery of gods embraced by the pagans; because of the clear-cut demands made by its code of life; because of the sharp outline of Jewish identity.

At the same time, in pagan states where religion and politics went hand-in-hand, kings who liked to encourage the belief that they were gods or at least of divine origin found the single-minded dedication to Yahweh alone as God a threat. Some Roman poets and historians made no secret of their contempt for Jews, for what they considered the barbarism of circumcision, for Jewish practices and customs.

Paul would preach and teach always out of his background as a Jew but his listeners were more and more people who neither understood nor sympathized with Judaism.

THE LAST YEARS (ACTS 21.15-28.31)

About the year 58, Paul decided to return to Jerusalem. James, the leader of the church there, was aware of the hostility that many Christians of Jewish background felt toward Paul. They considered him a destroyer of the laws and customs from the Jewish heritage that they still held sacred.

To show that this view of Paul was unfounded, James advised Paul to perform a ceremony of Jewish piety in the Temple itself. The ritual was connected with the completion of a specified time of service that one had vowed to God.

The gesture ended in disaster. Some who saw Paul in the Temple accused him of bringing his non-Jewish companions into an area forbidden to them by Jewish law. This was sacrilege. A riot broke out and Paul came dangerously close to being lynched until a detachment of Roman soldiers rescued him. Rescue and protective custody slipped into imprisonment as Paul remained a captive of the Romans. He was detained for a short time in Jerusalem and then transferred to Caesarea, the Mediterranean port about fifty miles northwest of Jerusalem.

As Paul's incarceration in Palestine dragged on for two years with no signs of a settlement, Paul exercised his privilege as a Roman citizen to appeal to the emperor in Rome for a judgment on his case.

In 61, Paul arrived in Rome. The conditions of his imprisonment there were loose enough so that for the two years it lasted, he was able to carry on a limited form of missionary activity. Here, the account in Acts leaves off.

What happened next is obscure. However, the traditional account of Paul's last years has him being released from the Roman arrest in 63. A journey to the East possibly followed. According to some sources, he also visited Spain, spreading there the message of Jesus. On his return to Rome, he suffered a second, harsher imprisonment during the persecution by the emperor, Nero.

Paul died a martyr's death in Rome, probably in 67.

WHY THIS BACKGROUND INFORMATION?

This brief discussion of letters and of Paul's life provides some hint of what went into the writing of Paul's letters. His Jewish background, with its theology, customs, laws. His contact with the culture and thought and civilization of Greece and Asia Minor. The discussions over the relationship between Judaism and Christianity. His experiences with the communities of Christians he encountered or founded. His travels and all that happened during them. The high spots and crises and friendships of his own personal life.

If we would know Paul, not simply as an historical figure writing dead letters, but as someone still proclaiming to us the magnificent truth about God and his love for us as shown in Jesus and the response expected to this love, we must be willing to make the effort to search out the riches of his words.

A PROFILE OF PAUL IN HIS OWN WORDS

Paul had his own ideas about who he was and what he was doing. The following passages from his letters may help us to know him better.

He had a clear idea of his role: 2 Corinthians 5.18-20
"All this has been done by God, who has reconciled us to himself through Christ and has given us the ministry of reconciliation. I mean that God, in Christ, was reconciling the world to himself, not counting men's transgressions against them, and that he has entrusted the message of reconciliation to us. This makes us ambassadors for Christ, God as it were appealing through us. We implore you, in Christ's name; be reconciled to God! "

He recognized that what he was doing was God's work:
2 Corinthians 3.4-6; 2 Corinthians 4.7
"This great confidence in God is ours, through Christ. It
is not that we are entitled of ourselves to take credit for
anything. Our sole credit is from God, who has made us
qualified ministers of a new covenant . . .
"This treasure we possess in earthen vessels to make it clear
that its surpassing power comes from God and not from us."

He considered his message true and authentic: Galatians 1.8
"For even if we, or an angel from heaven, should preach
to you a gospel not in accord with the one we delivered to
you, let a curse be upon him! "

His fidelity to his mission brought him much suffering:
See 2 Corinthians 11.24 ff., and note that after Paul has
listed all the physical suffering he has undergone, he ends
with these remarkable words, "Leaving other sufferings
unmentioned, there is that daily tension pressing on me,
my anxiety for all the churches. Who is weak that I am
not affected by it? Who is scandalized that I am not
aflame with indignation? "

*He was not afraid to assert his authority for the good of
the Church:* 1 Corinthians 4.19-21; 2 Corinthians 4.1-5
"But I shall come to you soon, the Lord willing, and find
out, not what they say, but what they can do . . .Which
do you prefer, that I come to you with a rod, or with love
and a gentle spirit? "

"Because we possess this ministry through God's mercy, we
do not give in to discouragement. Rather, we repudiate
shameful, underhanded practices. We do not resort to trick-
ery or falsify the word of God. We proclaim the truth
openly and commend ourselves to every man's conscience
before God . . .It is not ourselves we preach but Christ
Jesus as Lord, and ourselves as your servants for Jesus's
sake."

His intense convictions gave rise to strong feelings: 2 Corinthians 11.13-15, against preachers of false teachings "Such men are false apostles. They practice deceit in their disguise as apostles of Christ. And little wonder! For even Satan disguises himself as an angel of light. It comes as no surprise that his ministers disguise themselves as ministers of the justice of God. But their end will correspond to their deeds."

His overriding feeling for his communities is love: 1 Corinthians 4.14-16; 2 Corinthians 12.14-15 "I am writing you in this way not to shame you but to admonish you as my beloved children. Granted you have ten thousand guardians in Christ, you have only one father. It was I who begot you in Christ Jesus through my preaching of the gospel. I beg you, then, be imitators of me."

"This is the third time that I am about to visit you, and I am not going to burden you; for I do not want what you have, I only want you. Children should not save up for their parents, but parents for children. I will gladly spend myself and be spent for your sakes. If I love you too much, will I be loved the less for that? "

His wish for his people was peace and love: Philippians 1.9-10; Ephesians 4.1-3 "My prayer is that your love may more and more abound, both in understanding and wealth of experience, so that with a clear conscience and blameless conduct you may learn to value the things that really matter, up to the very day of Christ."

"I plead with you, then, as a prisoner for the Lord, to live a life worthy of the calling you have received, with perfect humility, meekness, and patience, bearing with one another lovingly. Make every effort to preserve the unity which has the Spirit as its origin and peace as its binding force."

A LIST OF PAUL'S LETTERS

	date	written from
1st to the Thessalonians (1 Thes)	51	Corinth
2nd to the Thessalonians (2 Thes)	51-52	Corinth
To the Galatians (Gal)	54-55 (or earlier)	Ephesus
To the Philippians (Phil)	56-57 (or 61-63 Rome)	Ephesus
1st to the Corinthians (1 Cor)	57	Ephesus
2nd to the Corinthians (2 Cor)	57	Macedonia
To the Romans (Rom)	57-58	Corinth
To Philemon (Phlm)	61-63	Rome
To the Colossians (Col)	61-63	Rome
To the Ephesians (Eph)	61-63	Rome
1st to Timothy (1 Tim)	65-67	Macedonia
Titus (Ti)	65-67	Macedonia
2nd to Timothy (2 Tim)	65-67	Rome

Of the above dates and places of origin for Paul's letters, some are certain, others are almost so, still others are hypotheses. The chart provides a convenient arrangement.

THE AUTHENTICITY OF PAUL'S LETTERS

"Authenticity," when used in reference to Books of the Bible, deals with the question of whether or not a work was really written by the person claimed as its author.

Thus, the Gospel of Matthew is authentic if it was written by the apostle, Matthew, who has been traditionally considered its author. The Letter of Paul to the Romans is authentic if that letter was actually written by Paul.

For many years, scholars have been weighing the characteristics of the letters attributed to Paul. They have studied language, style, theological ideas. They have considered the historical situations to which the letters seem to be addressed. They have asked and tried to answer questions like, "Could the issues being addressed in this letter possibly have existed in Paul's time, or are we sure that these issues only come much later:" (If the latter should be the case, then Paul could not have written that particular letter.) "Do the language and style of this letter square with the language and style of other letters? Are these two letters so different that they could not have been written by the same man? "

Practically all scholars will agree that the following letters were written by St. Paul:
1st Thessalonians
1st Corinthians
2nd Corinthians
Galatians
Philippians
Philemon
Romans

About the other letters, there is still a great deal of scholarly discussion. Despite the arguments that can be raised pro and con Paul's authorship, it seems unlikely that there will ever be proof satisfying enough to settle the question once and for all.

This must not keep anyone from reading all the letters and from treating them with the same respect.

If any of these letters were not actually written by Paul, then we are encountering a widespread custom of the time. Written documents were frequently presented as from some famous person so that the authority of that person might add weight to the document.

For example, the Book of Wisdom in the Old Testament reads as if it were the work of King Solomon. But Solomon reigned in the tenth century before Christ. The book was written in the first century before Christ. The real author wanted the prestige of the wise man, Solomon, to increase the appeal of his words.

Whatever the actual situation of authorship, all the letters in the New Testament are inspired. Inspiration refers to the fact that God was active and deeply involved in the production of these letters so that they might reveal to men the truth about God and themselves. Whatever the actual situation of authorship, all the letters are true, communicating to men of all times the wonder of God's love for them and calling forth from men the response of love and obedience to God.

SUGGESTIONS FOR REFLECTION

The questions at the end of these chapters serve a variety of purposes. Some are appropriate for discussion in a group; others are to refresh memory and highlight an idea in the reading; still others are for personal reflection after a prayerful reading of the Scriptures and this chapter. It is not necessary to answer all of the questions. Yet at times it is a help to read the questions before reading the chapter, and again after the reading . It is suggested that you peruse all the questions first, then select the ones appropriate for your occasion: Discussion, memory testing, prayerful self-reflection.

1. What are the advantages and limitations of letters for communicating? How are the same advantages and limitations present in Paul's epistles?

2. How can you see evidences of Paul's early personal background, family life, and upbringing reflected in his later mission?

3. How can we account for the dramatic personal change or conversion that occurred in Paul about the year 36? Have you ever heard of a similar religious experience in other persons? Have you ever experienced personally such a dramatic change from beyond yourself — from God — which changed the direction of your life?

4. Do you think an experience of personal conversion is necessary for a person to become fully a believer and preacher of the good news? Explain.

5. Paul was not often successful in converting fellow Jews to Jesus, but this did not cause him to lose heart. Instead he turned in his failure toward a creative new direction, converting the Gentiles. Have you ever experienced a seeming failure which you turned into a creative new thrust?

6. How did the early Church see its own continuity with Judaism? How did it see its uniqueness — different from being just another sect of Judaism?

7. Paul's Jewish background, studies, work, problems, dilemmas, travels, and friendships all played a role in his personal life mission. As you look back over your life story, how might such things have played a part in your formation as a Christian disciple today?

8. Reread the headings that characterize a profile of Paul in his own words. Reflect on each as to whether or not it characterizes you as a Christian, and rate yourself as 1 — High; 2 — Needs Improvement; 3 — Low.

9. What keeps religious people from becoming apostles? How can this be overcome?

10. After his conversion Paul's life was filled with adventures and some mishaps. Select one incident from these (e. g. shipwreck, stoning, speaking in synagogues, etc.) and imagine yourself in Paul's place. Where is it? Who is present? What are the issues involved? What are you suffering? How are you handling it?

CHAPTER II

PAUL, THE PASTOR OF CORINTH

This booklet will attempt to introduce the reader to Paul's
insights into God and man through a careful reading of
substantial portions of the First Letter to the Corinthians.
This guided reading will take into account what was said
in the first chapter.

If we would understand a letter written many years ago, we
must try to form a clear picture of the man who wrote; of
those to whom he was writing; of the reasons for his writing; of the world that swirled around him and his readers
and was taken for granted in correspondence.

We will continually recall that Paul was raised and trained as
a Jew; that he was familiar with Greek philosphy and culture; that he lived in cities that were important both in the
world of commerce and the world of ideas; that he was not
writing to a faceless, nameless crowd but to specific groups
and individuals whom he knew either in person or by report.

This particular booklet is entitled *Paul the Pastor* because
it shows Paul giving guidance, pastoral leadership, to a community of Christians personally known to him. This community was experiencing growing pains of various kinds.
Paul was asked to apply the remedy of advice and instruction.

The companion booklet is entitled *Paul the Theologian*
and is a comparable study of the Letter to the Romans.

This choice of titles does not imply that Paul stopped being a pastor when he was theologizing, or that he stopped being a theologian when he put on his pastor's hat. Paul was always both a pastor and a theologian. His directives about what to do and what not to do always flowed from his grasp of theology and his theology always led to practical decisions and actions.

But he was more obviously assuming a pastoral role when he wrote to the Corinthians struggling through the ups and downs of their new life as Christians. On the other hand, the Letter to the Romans is a superb, over-all view of what Jesus Christ, the Lord, is all about, written as a summary of Paul's mature reflection.

These two letters provide an intelligent introduction into Paul's insights into life's most crucial questions.

WHERE THE CORINTHIANS LIVED

Corinth is situated on the slender neck of land, about four miles wide, that keeps the region of Greece known as the Peloponnesus from being an island by joining it to the mainland. The city had a long and important history. By the time Paul walked its streets, it was already a century old in a new existence, rebuilt on the ruins of a previous, destroyed Corinth.

As can be seen on any map, a ship journey from one side of southern Greece to the other, hugging the shoreline as was the custom, was a matter of some 300 miles. Two hundred of those miles could be eliminated by getting ships across the narrow four miles that were the only obstacle in the way of a waterway between the Peloponnesus and the mainland. Expediting such a crossing was the chief occupation of Corinth. The canal, which does exist today, had not yet been dug. However, smaller ships could be dragged overland in a kind of channel built for them, while larger ships could be unloaded on one side of the isthmus and their cargoes hauled across to the other to be reloaded onto different ships. Corinth thus used two ports, one on each side of the ribbon of land.

Corinth had a high reputation for industry and shipbuilding. It kept a large population, possibly several hundreds of thousands, busy with all the affairs of a major commercial city. Its ports were frequented by sailors and businessmen from all parts of the Mediterranean world and beyond.

As a center for governmental administration, it boasted a high level of architecture and art. Of course, there were markets, shops, theaters for music and plays, sports centers. The impressive residences of the small wealthy class stood apart from the crowded and shabby tenements of the poor.

Corinth also had a reputation for immorality. Some of this was earned by the conduct of rootless people who came and went with ships and business and stopped only long enough to buy and sell and enjoy whatever pleasures the city might offer. But Corinth seemed to surpass even the usual expectations in the intensity of its immorality. In the speech of the time, a "Corinthian girl" was a standard way of referring to a prostitute. "To live like a Corinthian" meant to spend much time in the company of "Corinthian girls."

Some of this abandon might have been encouraged by the fact that the goddess of love, Aphrodite, was worshiped in a huge temple overlooking the city. If reports are true, one thousand priestesses were kept fully occupied in her service, which included ritual prostitution.

PAUL AT CORINTH

Paul visited Corinth early in the 50's. According to the account of that visit in Acts 18.1-18, Paul first lodged with two Jews who had become Christians in Rome, Aquila and Priscilla, and supported himself by his trade of tentmaker.

On the sabbaths, he went to the synagogue where he took advantage of the usual opportunity to give an explanation of the readings from the Hebrew Scriptures. In these homilies, he proclaimed Jesus as the Messiah to the Jews gathered for worship. When hostility to his message brought insult and opposition, Paul gave up the synagogue visits. He began teaching in the house of a man named Titus Justus. Titus was a Gentile who had embraced Judaism's one God and the basic morality that this God demanded without adopting all the Jewish ritual and laws.

As Paul's efforts began to meet with some success, he prolonged his stay.

Eventually, his Jewish adversaries went to the local Roman official, Gallio, and accused Paul of breaking laws when he taught. Gallio dismissed the Jewish charge with the observation that he had no intention of getting involved in religious squabbles.

After a year and a half at Corinth, Paul departed leaving behind a fairly substantial community of new Christians; some Jews, more non-Jews, mostly from the working and slave portions of the population.

FURTHER DEVELOPMENTS AT CORINTH

About four or five years passed between the time Paul left Corinth and the writing of this letter, from the city of Ephesus about 56 or 57. What had happened in the meantime?

Acts 18 tells of a man named Apollos, "a native of Alexandria and a man of eloquence . . . He was both an authority on Scripture and instructed in the new way of the Lord. Apollos was a man full of spiritual fervor." This Apollos traveled in Greece and "was vigorous in his public refutation of the Jewish party as he went about establishing from the Scriptures that Jesus is the Messiah."

This impressive man came to Corinth and obviously made his mark there.

Much more had also been going on. Questions multiplied for the group still struggling for Christian identity. How should Christians act in the midst of the paganism and immorality around them? How should they deal with what seemed out of line in their own community? How should they come to terms with the new and different ideas being discussed in their gatherings for liturgy and prayer?

A delegation was sent to Paul to get his instructions. But there was a complication. Certain groups at Corinth were not willing to accept Paul and what he might say. To them, his credentials and authority to teach them were second-rate. They gave no weight to Paul's advice.

Paul received news about Corinth from two different sources. One source was the delegation bringing the official request for Paul's help, "Stephanas, Fortunatus and Achaicus," mentioned in 1 Corinthians 16.17. Members of the household of a woman named Chloe (1.11) brought Paul other news. His right to intervene in the affairs of the church at Corinth was being questioned and undermined.

Before Paul took up the issues referred to him by the official delegation (chapter 5 and following), he decided to bring up the dangerous divisions he saw arising among the Christians at Corinth.

PAUL'S GREETING TO THE CORINTHIANS: 1.1-3

Paul was writing a letter. He followed the style of letters of his time. We generally begin our letters, "Dear . . ." In Paul's day, the greeting was much more informative. It included the name of the writer, the names of those to whom he was writing, a more or less elaborate formula of greeting.

Paul identifies himself as "called by God's will to be an

apostle of Christ Jesus." The stories of the calls of the great men of God make up a significant part of the Old Testament. Moses is called, as is Abraham, the prophets and many others. The call stories emphasize that these men were chosen by God to play a special role in his activities for his people.

Paul describes himself as one of this distinguished line of God's servants, one who is aware that God has chosen him for a special work.

That special work is to be an "apostle." The name, "apostle," generally associated with the special twelve that Jesus chose, has a broader meaning for Paul. An "apostle" is, literally, "one who is sent." For Paul, the qualifications of an apostle are that he has seen the Risen Lord, that he has been called and sent by him to preach the message of Jesus' death and resurrection and that in his own life he imitates the death and resurrection of Jesus.

Paul considers himself an apostle. He has had an experience of the Lord and has been sent by him to preach the Good News. The reason he insists on this title for himself is not that he is hungry for dignity but that he knows that some Corinthians who will be reading his letter have been making little of him. He asserts his authority and displays his credentials to write and to be heeded.

Paul writes to the "church of God which is in Corinth." The word, "church," (in Greek *ekklesia,* from the words, "called from," "convoked") identifies the Christians as those who have been called together by the Father around a common faith in the Lord Jesus Christ. The way Paul uses the word, "church," is worth noticing. The emphasis is not on a Church which is the sum total of many "churches." Rather, each community, however small, represents, and is, the Church in the locale in which it exists and operates.

The group of Christians at Corinth is the Church in so far

as it will touch the lives of people living in those days, walking those streets, taken up in that business which was Corinth.

Paul affirms that the community of believers, the Church, is called to be "holy." "Holy," in the language of the Bible, is the distinctive attribute of God. It specifies God as set apart, separated from, the human condition. Men die. God is Life. Men are limited in their talents and strength. God is Power and Knowledge. Men sin, are caught by evil. God is Good.

To his kind of life God has called men. To show that they have entered this new Life that belongs to God himself, something drastic must happen to the way men live.

Paul greets the Christians at Corinth with the salutation, "Grace and peace."

GRACE

"Grace" is God's good will, love, generosity to men. This good will and love go beyond mere feeling. Much good feeling toward people never gets translated into tangible deeds. No practical action springs from mere feeling. God's love is a very — to speak paradoxically — down-to-earth thing. Unlike men who may feel "love" without many results, God makes his love and care evident. He acts through men to free them from the evil and sin that smothers them. This love is uniquely demonstrated in the life and death and resurrection of Jesus. God's becoming man is the surest proof of the depth of God's love. This is the greatest grace.

"Grace" also includes all those signs in the life of individuals and the community which attract others to recognize and be drawn to God's presence. Such signs are "love, joy, peace, patient endurance, kindness, generosity, faith, mildness and chastity" (Gal 5.22-23). Paul wishes for the Cor-

25

inthians that they will be open to recognize and receive
God's love for them in all the situations where this love
is demonstrated.

PEACE

"Peace" is a very broad term referring to what happens
when all is as it should be according to the will of God.
Peace exists when man is right with God, with himself, with
other men, with all creation. Peace is the ultimate state
where all these relationships are in divinely ordered harmony permanently and perfectly. Peace is also the state
of mind of the person who knows that he is doing his
best to cooperate with God's plan now and believes that
despite the obvious failures here and now, the plan will
without any doubt be carried out.

PAUL'S GREETING

A paraphrase of the main ideas in Paul's greeting might go
something like this:

"I, Paul, have been called by God. I am an apostle because I have met in a privileged way Jesus who died and
rose again. I have been sent by him to bring to others the
secret of life's meaning. Because God, for his own reasons,
has seen fit to choose me, I have the authority to write
to you, the Christians at Corinth.

"You, too, have been called by God to make real and vital
his presence where you live and work by the depth of your
faith and the quality of your lives.

"I pray that you will recognize and accept from God all
good things that he offers, especially his Son, Jesus Christ,
and his constant presence in signs around us. Rejoice in
the knowledge that the future belongs to God and you."

SUGGESTIONS FOR REFLECTION

1. What does it mean to be a pastor?   How is this different from being a theologian?   Does it make a difference which one is predominantly?   Can one person be both?

2. Locate Corinth on a map.   Why is it important to know what the Corinthians and life in Corinth were like?   How can the epistle still apply to us today?

3. Factions cause great problems in the Body of Christ which is the Church.   In your life or historical memory recall a dangerous division among Christians.   What was its effect on those involved and on those outside it?

4. Paul identifited himself as an "apostle," i. e., "one who was called by God for a special role or work to proclaim Jesus, and give meaning for the lives of fellow Christians." With this definition in mind, why should every Christian be able to call himself an "apostle? " If every member of the Christian community saw himself and the others as called in this way, could there be factions or divisions in the Church?

CHAPTER III

"WISDOM" AND
THE DANGEROUS DIVISION

Please read: 1 Corinthians 1. 10-4. 2

Recent experience may help us appreciate what had been
happening at Corinth.

With official approval of more variety in liturgy, Catholics
have expressed their preference for various styles of liturgy
— folk Mass vs. more traditional music; singing vs. non-sing-
ing; English vs. Latin. Choices are also being made for or
against the priest on account of his style of liturgical
celebration or his preaching. Rectories have gotten accus-
tomed to parishioners phoning to ask, "What Masses will
Father X have tomorrow? "

These preferences are backed up by attendance at those
liturgies which affect one more deeply, and by non-atten-
dance at those which have little appeal. Many Catholics feel
free to go to parishes other than their own if they discover
liturgies and preachers more suited to their needs.

Something similar was occurring at Corinth. Some people
associated themselves more directly with Paul; others with
the eloquent preacher, Apollos; still others with Peter, whose
contact with Corinth is still not clear. There was also a
"Christ-group."

In and by itself, there is nothing wrong or even surprising
in the inevitable fact that the manner or language or personality of one minister will prove more attractive to some
than to others. The danger arises when the attraction to

28

preachers or leaders causes real factions in the community, when the association with one religious personality means separation from and rivalry with others.

This had not yet happened in Corinth. But, if events continued the way they were going, it might have. Hence, Paul tried to remind the Corinthians what being a Christian is all about.

"WISDOM," THE SLOGAN

Just as "guitars," or "Latin," or "relevance" have developed into slogans around which armies have formed for modern liturgical contests and just as "original sin" or "Jesus' knowledge" or "virgin birth" have sparked theological controversy (even among those who were puzzled about what exactly was being discussed), "wisdom" was a key word in the church of Corinth.

Some Corinthians were convinced that they had reached such a depth of maturity in Christian knowledge, such a richness of insight, such a closeness to God, that they stood far above the common herd of Christians, including Paul. They had wisdom.

The word, "wisdom," rang a bell with both Gentiles and Jews.

For those acquainted with Greek philosophy, wisdom was the harmony and plan of the universe. There was an all-embracing direction to the movement of man and the universe. Man could be wise only if he tried to discover this plan and fit his own life into it. The way to know this plan was to use natural abilities and talents. Long hours in reflection on life and the universe would bring the answers. Of course, one did not have to find all the answers himself. He could and should listen to the wise men of his own and previous times, be moved by their insights and by the artistry of their speech and writing. The truly wise man moved smoothly and easily with the irresistible thrust of the universe that his study and reflection revealed.

The Jew also saw wisdom as the way to live but he gained wisdom more by listening to God's directions than by philosophy and study. For the Jew, the privileged expression of the correct way of life was the Jewish Law; the commandments, the laws that interpreted the commandments, the traditions that interpreted the laws.

Each of these quests for wisdom was good in its own way. Each shared the same danger.

They were good because they asked man to look beyond the present moment and the satisfaction of his (its) needs and desires and to make the present moment part of a greater, more noble design.

They were open to danger because both could leave the impression that as man deepened his knowledge of the plan of the universe, or of God's will, he would necessarily move closer to and mesh better with that vast power that ruled all. In other words, knowledge itself was the key to a deeper sharing in the life of the Infinite.

There is some truth to this, but for Paul, man needs not only to know God intellectually but to recognize and live by dependence on him. To emphasize too much what man can do by his own talents, his own thought processes, is to be open to the danger that as man grows taller, God grows shorter, at least in man's estimation. Once this fatal deception takes place, man is reduced to nothing because his true worth comes from what he is in relation to God who created him to share with God himself the rule of creation.

WISDOM IN THE CHRISTIAN EXPERIENCE AT CORINTH

To show how the Christians with swelled heads over their

wisdom should have known better, Paul reminded them of their own experience. This experience should have demonstrated how little merely human talent and intelligence and wisdom had counted at Corinth.

The *message* preached could in no way qualify as "wisdom" (1.18-25). The message was Jesus crucified – absolute nonsense to both Greeks and Jews. Nonsense to Greeks because a dead man on a cross in no way measured up to their illusions of a sublime plan for the universe. What could a crucified Jew offer to compare with the riches of Aristotle and Socrates and their other great thinkers! Nonsense to the Jews because their Law declared that anyone who hung on a cross was cursed. How could a cursed man be part of God's dealings with them?

The *class of people* who received the Christian message at Corinth was not usually associated with wisdom (1.26-31). Not scholars or philosophers or patrons of the arts, not "beautiful people," the believers at Corinth were "the lowborn and despised," mostly slaves and manual laborers, or perhaps at best, skilled craftsmen and small shopowners.

Paul himself was not a great advertisement for wisdom (2.1-5). He did not consider himself a persuasive speaker, nor an eloquent orator. He says that he wasn't beyond nervousness when he had to speak to the Corinthians.

TRUE WISDOM

For Paul, Jesus Christ is the only true wisdom. His death and resurrection reveal life's meaning. No one reaches this meaning by the brute resources of human thought itself, nor is anyone able to accept it because it makes such good sense. God's guidance is essential. Only when God opens a man's eyes and heart can he begin to understand and appreciate what God has done and is doing.

The trouble with the Corinthians is that they claim to have

true wisdom and yet the squabbling over considerations of merely human wisdom gives the lie to their claim (3.1-4).

THE ROLE OF MEN IN GOD'S WORK

Once there is clear recognition that only God can make known the plan of the universe and bring men to accept it, there should be no problem about seeing how those whom he chooses to be his instruments fit into his plan. Each one so chosen makes his own particular contribution. The value of that contribution cannot be denied. At the same time, without the all-pervasive action of God making that work effective, nothing could happen.

Paul, using an image from farming, explains what happened at Corinth. As the first preacher there, he planted the seed. Apollos, by his skilled and polished presentations, drew out for the Corinthians the significance of Jesus Christ and so watered the seed that Paul had planted. But only the constant care of God caused the work of Paul and Apollos to bear fruit in the hearts of the Corinthians. And only God can be the judge of how much any man's work has accomplished — not those smug and pompous Corinthians who are so eager to write Paul off as second-rate.

THE CHURCH AS THE TEMPLE OF GOD (3. 16-17)

Moving from an illustration taken from farming, Paul turns to another example to convey how he understands the Church. The local church is the "temple of God." In the Hebrew Scriptures, the Temple is the place where the unseen God makes himself present. No one can see God as he is. At the same time, there has to be some way to relate to this mysterious, seemingly absent God.

One relates to an absent friend through a letter or through photos. The friend becomes present in the words which are symbols for face-to-face contact or in the photos.

In the belief of the Israelites, God was present in the

Temple at Jerusalem. God was in the Temple because he chose to be, and he was there more intimately than he was in creation, for example. But he was also so tremendous that his presence could never be limited to any one place or situation or action. Places, situations, and actions could reveal God but never totally, even if one put them all together.

On Israel's part, to take the belief about God's presence seriously included the obligation of coming to the place of his presence with integrity. Anyone meeting God in the symbols of worship had to reflect that meeting in the words and activities of life. Anything else was hypocrisy.

When Paul writes, "You are the temple of God," he is insisting that just as the Israelites of old and the Jews of his day met God in the Temple, from then on all men ought to be able to meet God in the life of the Christian community.

God's presence in a building has been surpassed by God's presence in the living community of believers. Their behavior should let the life of God shine through.

The teachers in the community can so mar and deface the life of the community that it becomes impossible to recognize God there. In this case, the Temple, the sign of God's presence in a locality, is effectively destroyed. To this, Paul says, "If anyone destroys God's temple, God will destroy him."

Paul lays on the line a dreadful possibility he foresees for Corinth. The quibbling over groups, over the attachment to one leader or another, could grow so serious that the church there ceases to be a sign of God's love and unity. Then the community will be in ruins, as the Jerusalem Temple had been reduced to burned and battered rubble in 587 B. C. And woe to those who might be responsible for this!

In passing, it should be noted that nowhere does Paul have a bad word for Apollos. Evidently Apollos was not trying to build up a fan club opposed to Paul's. The enthusiasm for one teacher over another was not encouraged by either Apollos or Paul.

DIVISIONS TODAY

Paul has begun this letter with a defense of his own authority, his own right to challenge and judge the conduct of the Corinthians. Before he can respond to practical questions posed to him, he must deal with a potentially destructive underlying attitude spreading at Corinth. This is to make too much of the personality, the preaching skills, the learning of those who have formed the community at Corinth. It also makes too much of man's power to lift himself by his own bootstraps to save his world. The result is that the burden of sin and the work of God and Jesus to relieve men of it are bound to be underplayed.

Without denying that God reaches to the world through the qualities and talents of humans, Paul tries to correct the abuse of overestimating these gifts.

They are being overestimated when they become such a preoccupation that the harmony and unity of the congregation are destroyed. In this case, the community ceases to function in its most sublime role, as the place where, through unity and love, the presence of God is felt.

Not too much imagination is needed to discern the principles that so badly need to be applied to the life of the Church today.

Plurality, diversity are a necessary and natural part of the life of the community. But when is plurality and diversity the sign of the many facets of God and when is it a destroying Babel caused by proud men?

What constitutes authority in the Church? "Each man his own authority" is nonsense. At the same time, simply to have a position of authority because of having completed so many years of study or having been appointed to it is not enough. Authorities, leaders, like Paul the apostle, will count for most when their lives reflect the death and resurrection of Jesus.

No generation, no chain of generations, will ever change the world without God. At the same time, God calls and directs men to work with him. Where do we fit in, as individuals, as the members of the Christian community?

SUGGESTIONS FOR REFLECTION

1. Let three persons each take a role and strongly defend its position toward the liturgy today:
Role 1 — "I favor the guitar Mass on Sundays."
Role 2 — "I wish the Latin would be resumed at Mass."
Role 3 — "I only attend Mass when the liturgy is relevant to my life."
Then, using Paul's reasoning in this letter, let the three participants try to resolve the dilemna these positions foster.

2. "Wisdom" was:
for the Greeks — Philosophical speculation on the plan and harmony of the universe.
for the Jews — following God's directions for life — the commandments.
How would you describe "Wisdom" for our times?

3. Paul claimed that "Wisdom" is a Person — Jesus Christ crucified, seeming nonsense and foolishness. What meaning has this for our times and history? Take several important persons in the news; i. e., the Holy Father, the President, your Bishop, the Leader of a Movement, etc., and evaluate the mission of each as it might relate to Paul's idea of "Wisdom."

4. What meaning has Paul's idea of "Wisdom" for your life right now?

5. Sometimes we tend to treat personalities unfavorably when resolving an issue. At no time did Paul ever condemn or downplay Apollos as a person. Take a sample issue in the news today (i. e., housing, taxes, churchgoing, etc.) and use Paul's style of argument through the issue rather than through persons.

6. In your home or parish, or business, give examples similar to Paul's illustration that in God's work Paul planted, Apollos watered, and someone else did the reaping.

7. Sometimes Paul's failures or limitations became successful in the long run because God was ultimately behind them. Has this ever happened in your life?

8. As a parent or religion teacher describe an instance where the children were divided into factions. How could you have found answers for them in this epistle?

CHAPTER IV

BORN FREE?

Probably nothing is a more noble aspiration of man than
freedom. Probably nothing is used to justify more abuse
and nonsense than "freedom."

People don't change all that much. Refashion the clothes;
remove the cars and replace them with horses, donkeys and
carts; modify the style and height of the buildings and you
might be hard-pressed to distinguish whether the masses of
humanity were rushing along the streets of Corinth or those
of New York, London or Moscow.

In that mass of humanity will be those who are genuinely
oppressed by the system in which they live. In that mass
of humanity will be those who are beginning to taste freedom. In that mass of humanity will be those who feel that
their personal freedom places them above the usual restraints
of society or law. In that mass of humanity will be those
who are shocked by the excesses they believe are being
committed in the name of freedom.

THE CASE: EATING MEAT

Please read: 1 Corinthians 8-10

Except in the old days of fish on Friday, eating meat would
cause no great conscience problems for Catholics. Now-
adays, the problem is more likely to be financial than
moral — how often can a family afford that roast?

In Paul's days, the situation was more complicated.

Great civic holidays involved religious celebration. Although how much real belief in the gods was involved is questionable, traditional rituals were observed as a matter of course. On such festive days, a common practice was the sacrifice of animals.

The same was true for personal occasions that one wanted to mark in high fashion. The sacrifice of oxen or other animals to a god was often part of the festivities of a birthday, the beginning or end of a trip, some successfully concluded business venture.

When the prescribed ceremonial for the slaughter of the animal had been properly observed, there generally followed a feast in which the main course was the meat from the animal sacrificed. This meal signified union with the god to whom the animal had been offered. It also showed that those who shared the meal were joined together by some common bond.

The basic idea is not too different from great holiday gatherings in our own days. Families and friends come together on occasions like Christmas, Thanksgiving, weddings. The meal eaten during the festivities is not just a matter of filling the belly but is a sign that this is one family, or a group of friends. This holds true even when those same people don't see one another for the rest of the year. Even relatives who have no special liking for one another seem to feel that they ought to get together for this meal for the sake of "togetherness."

As harmless and commonplace as this all sounds, what should not be forgotten is that the meal in Paul's time had a religious dimension. Those who shared the meal had to take into account that somehow a god was involved in what they were doing.

On special occasions, the sacrificial slaughter reached grand proportions. Ten or fifty oxen are tons of meat. Often,

there just weren't enough people or big enough appetites
to do away with all that beef. When this happened, the
meat was sold cheaply to butchers who in their turn resold
it at bargain prices. This meant that the poor had a chance
for a steak dinner.

THE SURFACE PROBLEM

What appears like good cheer and a break for the poor hid
a conscience problem for some Christians.

As was indicated previously, the meat had been offered to
a god or goddess. To eat of the meal could be taken as
at least a nod to that world of pagan deities on which the
Christian Corinthians had turned their backs. To share the
dinner arranged by a friend or relative in thanks for the
birth of a son, when that dinner included sacrifice to a
pagan god, could compromise strong faith in one God.

Even an invitation to an ordinary dinner could be suspect.
Suppose the Christian were asked to the home of a friend
whose finances usually allowed nothing more than a dish
of farina and a chunk of bread. Now, for this supper, the
table is crowned with a standing rib roast. Could the Christian not suspect that this prosperity was not prosperity at
all but a purchase made from meat sold cheaply because it
had first been offered in sacrifice?

In these situations, could the Christian eat the meat?   Would
his eating be looked upon as weakness in his allegiance to
the one true God?   Could the meal be separated from
associations with pagan religion?

THE DEEPER PROBLEM

This problem hardly stirs interest any more. It seems to
be an historical curiosity with not much to say to us.

Not so!

Beyond this eating or not eating meat lies a serious, always pressing issue — the use of freedom.

At Corinth, there were those who believed that they had "knowledge." Through special insights given to them by the Spirit, they had a right understanding of this whole issue of meals and pagan gods.

Pagan gods do not exist. There is only the one true God. Therefore, the food offered to the pagan gods is offered to no God. This being the case, there is absolutely no reason why the Christians should not eat the food. Nothing has happened to it. Nothing has been done to it. All that has taken place is an empty and pointless rite.

Perfectly logical, perfectly correct reasoning. But not quite complete.

What is not taken into account is that there are other people to be considered. What effect will the sight of a Christian feasting at a pagan religious meal have on other guests or onlookers?

There were at Corinth those whom Paul called the "weak." This term he used with sympathy for the Christians who could not break loose from the training and habits of years. No matter what they might be told, they still were so formed that when they saw a Christian eating sacrificed meat, they were scandalized. For them, such conduct compromised faith in God.

This is not difficult to appreciate. Catholics who had grown up, lived their middle years and passed into old age with "no meat on Friday" often found it hard to accept the fact that they now saw gentlemen in Roman collars slicing into a steak on Friday.

No matter what the mind may try to accept, it's not easy to write off long-standing attitudes. And sometimes even the

mind cannot accept changes in beliefs and practices that it
has taken for granted for as long as it can remember.

For Paul, the real issue at Corinth was not simply, "Is it
wrong for me to eat food offered to pagan gods? " Much
more important was, "If I eat food that has been offered,
what will I do to those who see me eating? "

Paul's concern is that one who believes that such feasting
is wrong may see another Christian taking part and, even
though his conscience tells him that it's wrong, he might be
induced to eat also. In that case, what is not wrong for the
one who does not believe it to be so becomes wrong for the
one who thinks he is doing wrong.

In Paul's own words, "If someone sees you, with your
'knowledge,' reclining at table in the temple of an idol, may
not his conscience in its weak state be influenced to the
point that he eats the idol-offering? Because of your 'knowledge' the weak one perishes, that brother for whom Christ
died. When you sin thus against your brothers and wound
their weak consciences, you are sinning against Christ"
(8.10-12).

Paul's answer to the question moves not into fine points of
theological expertise but to an intensely personal conclusion.
"Therefore, if food causes my brother to sin I will never
eat meat again, so that I may not be an occasion of sin to
him."

Paul has moved to the broader and perennial challenge of
the use of freedom. What limits are there to one's acting
the way he chooses when he is convinced that he is right?

PAUL'S OWN EXAMPLE (CHAPTER 9)

"I beg you, then, be imitators of me" (1 Cor 4.16).
"Imitate me as I imitate Christ" (1 Cor 11.1).

Statements like these are strong stuff. Colossal nerve to tell people to "live like me, because I live like Christ." Or magnificent holiness.

Paul believed he brought Jesus' message not only in the words he preached but also in the way he lived. This was one of the proofs that he was truly an apostle.

Paul used his own experience to give the Corinthians an example of freedom at work.

As an apostle, Paul was entitled to the rights of an apostle. One of those rights was support from those to whom he preached. This was not a new idea. Provision for the traveling Jewish teachers seems to have been discussed among the rabbis. Itinerant Greek "philosophers," many of them phonies of the first order, expected payment for rolling their pearls of wisdom into the town square.

Paul marshals arguments to back up his right to have his material needs provided. From common experience: the soldier gets paid for his work; the farmer eats the grapes of his vineyard; the shepherd drinks the milk of his flock. From Jewish tradition: those who work in the Temple in Jerusalem receive what they need; even oxen can take mouthfuls of the grain they are threshing. From Christian tradition and practice: the others who work for the Church receive support; a saying of Jesus himself authorizes this.

When his argument has been clearly established and Paul, with every right, could have asked the people of Corinth to supply what he needed, he said, "I have never used any of these rights." His reason for this unusual behavior? That nothing in his life be open to suspicion, that there be not even the faintest hint that he is a missionary preacher for material benefit, that his conduct place no obstacle in any way to the effectiveness of his preaching.

Paul was free to use the right that was his according to common sense and precedent. But he had a greater freedom,

the freedom to give up this right if it might hinder his
mission to preach the gospel.

Paul moves from this to explain his missionary attitude.

He says that when he worked among the Jews still observ-
ing the laws of Judaism, he kept those laws himself. When
he lived among the Gentiles who felt no obligation to Jewish
customs and regulations, he felt free from their observance.
When he dealt with the "weak," with those whose consciences
were still poorly formed and who saw certain patterns of
behavior necessary that were not really so, Paul acted in
accord with their expectations. Paul sums up, "I have made
myself all things to all men."

Paul was doing what today's jargon would call, "meeting
people where they are." The good news of Jesus had to
reach these people at the particular level to which their
own development had brought them.

Paul was so free that he was able to discern that many issues
that seemed so important to these groups meant nothing
at all in the long run. The only important consideration
for him in deciding on his own course of action was to
avoid placing unnecessary obstacles to his word being heard.

Paul was not a chameleon who changed colors to fit his environ-
ment. He was not an unprincipled man willing to pretend to
anything in order to register more names in his convert book.

Paul was a free man who recognized what was a matter of
principle and what was not. When principle was involved,
Paul would not bend. Examples are numerous where he
draws lines, raises challenges, refuses to compromise, speaks
straightforwardly no matter what the result.

But when the matter was not one of principle, he would
put tremendous demands on himself to make his life and
behavior as acceptable as he could to the people he was trying to reach.

THE MEAT DISPUTE: FINAL ANSWERS

From the principles he has presented, Paul is able to give specific direction to the Corinthians.

1. Do not take part in a meal which is explicitly and directly intended as a religious ceremony in honor of the gods. Even though there are no "gods," to take part in a pagan ritual meal is to become involved in a world which is hostile to the one true God.

2. When buying meat in the butcher shops, do not bother to question whether or not the meat was offered in sacrifice.

3. If you are invited to dinner with unbelievers and are served meat, you need not ask whether the meat was offered to idols.

4. If, in the same situation, another diner points out that the meat at the feast was part of a pagan sacrifice, then do not eat the meat for fear of giving bad example.

5. The over-riding rule is, "No man should seek his own interest but rather that of his neighbor" (1 Cor 11.26).

ANOTHER PROBLEM IN THE USE OF FREEDOM—
WOMEN IN CHURCH

Please read: 1 Corinthians 11. 2-16

This section could be an embarrassment. Paul seems to get tangled in feminine fashions, stirring up a tempest in a beauty parlor. More serious, Paul's words seem to qualify him for the list of Most Wanted Male Chauvinists. After all, Paul writes that a woman ought to wear a head veil at the liturgy while a man ought to keep his head uncovered. Paul says that man is a reflection of God's glory while woman is a reflection of man's glory since woman was made from and created for man.

However, closer consideration shows that Paul doesn't deserve all the abuse he has been taking recently.

The issues at stake are, "Does Paul really state the superiority of men over women? " "If he does say something that sounds like this, is it a matter of changeless theological truth or a reflection of the social customs of the time? "

Some information about these customs may be helpful here.

GREEK CUSTOMS

What women's styles were in the lands influenced by Greek culture is not absolutely clear. According to Paul's own statements, short hair was apparently the rule for men. Long hair was considered a sign of effeminacy. This would have been a reversal of the usual fashion and perhaps lasted for only a short time.

Although customs varied from place to place, it was more common for women to wear their hair long and to cover their heads with veils when they went out of the house.

However, when attending the sometimes rather wild religious rites of what are known as the "mystery religions," women let their hair hang loose, i. e., not tied or held in place by ribbons or nets, and wore no hats or veils.

Among the Greeks, then, there were customs governing the use or non-use of head coverings and accepted hair styles. But these had nothing to do with the superiority of men and inferiority of women. They were a matter of what was considered proper and decent.

JEWISH CUSTOMS

Among the Jews, there were demanding rules for women, as well as for men.

Jewish women, at least in the Jewish homeland, kept a low

profile in public life. Whenever a Jewess left her home, her head and face were hidden by a complicated arrangement of veils, hairbands and ribbons. Any woman who appeared in public without so decking herself out committed such a breach of good taste that her husband had the right, even the duty, to divorce her.

At religious services, women were not allowed to read the Scriptures aloud in the synagogue, nor to teach, as the men were. Women were there to listen and to learn.

Some scholars have noted that there is evidence to suggest that the reason for head covering, at least within the context of religious services, was that, granting the attitudes of the times, a woman's hair and face would have been distracting, perhaps even seductive to men. The rules might have been intended to prevent problems in this area at the synagogue service.

WHY PAUL GETS INVOLVED

Paul goes into complicated arguments about why women should wear their hair long and have their heads covered.

The Genesis story of creation is introduced. Verses 3 and 7-9 depend on the creation account. Christ, not mentioned in the Genesis account but taken for granted by Paul as the one through whom God created, was the source of the first man. The man, in turn, was the source of the woman — the rib story. Man is a manifestation of God, showing in himself some of the qualities of God, whereas woman, created from man, manifests the qualities of man.

Paul also appeals to the fact that women actually do wear long hair and veils and that this is the prevailing custom in the Christian communities.

Paul's more significant concern is the same as that expressed in the previous meat question — the responsible use of freedom.

Some women had heard the Christian message. They had been taught that to accept Jesus means liberty, freedom. For them, "I am free" was equivalent to "I do what I please."

The women, exercising their freedom, had been coming to liturgical celebrations with their hair flowing free and uncovered. In itself, there was nothing wrong with this. But Christians of Jewish background were being scandalized because, for them, uncovered head and loose hair indicated a woman who grossly disregarded social convention. Christians of pagan background were disturbed because, for them, loose hair and uncovered head carried too many overtones of the wild ceremonies of the pagan mystery religions.

Paul wants the women to consider his rule for the use of freedom, "No man should seek his own interest but rather that of his neighbor."

Paul evidently believed that the new fashion was harmful. The particular freedom involved in being able to toss off the conventions of head dress is so minor in proportion to the uproar being caused that Paul can only come to the conclusion that the women ought to conform to custom.

This leads to further questions. What is Paul's attitude toward women?

As for freedom, is the burden always on the one who is more advanced, more progressive, to give in to the lack of openness of those set in their ways? Don't those people also have the obligation to be more open to new and different ways if they're not wrong? Must we always do things the way we always did them for fear of hurting someone's feelings?

PAUL AND WOMEN

There is a tension in Paul's attitude toward women. At times, he seems to write of them as inferior to men.

"Women should keep silent in such [liturgical] gatherings. They may not speak. Rather, as the law states, submissiveness is indicated for them. If they want to learn anything, they should ask their husbands at home. It is a disgrace when a woman speaks in the assembly" (1 Cor 14.34-35).

On the other hand, in the very passage we have just been considering, in 1 Corinthians 11, Paul emphasizes equality and mutual interdependence of man and woman. "Yet, in the Lord, woman is not independent of man nor man independent of woman. In the same way that woman was made from man, so man is born of woman; and all is from God" (11.11-12). According to Galatians 3.28, "There does not exist among you Jew or Greek, slave or freeman, male or female. All are one in Christ Jesus."

We might sum up Paul's attitude to women as follows:

1. Paul, a man of his time, accepts some social customs, some distinctions between men and women which include attitudes of subordination of woman to man.

2. Paul, deeply influenced by his faith, holds the theological position that all, men and women, are equal before God. For Paul, this is not just a pious nod to theology to be forgotten in the nitty-gritty where women are inferior. A careful reading of Paul shows a progressive attitude to women that comes from his theological understanding. Many of his statements of practical conduct place man and woman on the same footing.

3. Paul sees this world as a passing reality. The real world is that which is in the process of being created under the rule of Jesus Christ. Christians need not waste time trying to change social structures in this already decaying sinful situation. Rather, they should try to recognize their relationship with Jesus and try to live out that relationship.

If they do this, any unjust institutions will wither of their own inherent sickness.

Another instance of this point of view can be found in the Letter to Philemon. This brief epistle was written by Paul about a runaway slave, Onesimus, who had come to Paul and been converted by him. The runaway was persuaded by Paul to return to Philemon, his master, also a Christian.

A shocking example of Paul selling out to establishment evils?

This is how Paul wrote to the slave owner: "Perhaps he was separated from you for a while for this reason: that you might possess him forever, no longer as a slave but as more than a slave, a beloved brother, especially dear to me; and how much more than a brother to you, since now you will know him both as a man and in the Lord" (Phlm 15-16).

The Christians, an insignificant band of powerless people, many of them slaves themselves, lacked the influence to change the entrenched system of slavery. Whatever little agitation they might have been capable of would probably have been considered a slave rebellion with horrible punishment a distinct possibility.

Philemon, if he listens to Paul's request that he receive back his slave as "a beloved brother" known "both as a man and in the Lord," can hardly oppress him or treat him badly.

The most effective and lasting remedy for any injustice begins within the hearts of men. Laws and customs change as a matter of course after internal transformation.

Although we would probably insist that both these avenues be walked simultaneously, i. e., changing man from within and changing institutions by regulation, we have had enough experience to know that changes in laws and institutions do not accomplish everything. Laws outlawing discrimination have been on the books for years. Despite this, society still harbors discrimination. There is still lacking the inner conviction that Paul insisted on, that people must believe in their hearts that they are all one in Jesus Christ before they will treat one another as God intended.

IN THE MATTER OF FREEDOM, WHO HAS TO GIVE IN?

When freedom clashes with established ways, which gives in?

Suppose as a priest, I like my hair very long to match my flowing beard and set off my purple clerical shirt. Suppose this bothers most of my parishioners who are elderly middle Americans.

My clothes and hair style are not important. Why can't the people get used to them? Does my message and the holiness of my life depend on my looking like a Wall Street broker in black?

A good question — and not easy to answer. Paul has given us the principles. Clothes and hair style are not important. I am free to wear what I choose. What is important is that the minister preach the word of Jesus and imitate his life.

However, I should be so free that for the greater good of being able to reach people more effectively, I can cut my hair, shave my beard and wear clerical black. Perhaps, once that obstacle is gotten over, we can get to the business of what is really important for a Christian and a priest.

But suppose some people are absolutely wedded to the idea that the essence of Christianity is respectable clothing and traditional grooming. Then perhaps I am justified in what might seem a bizarre appearance as a way of challenging the values of those who cannot be reached in any other way.

50

This example shows the complexity of the use of freedom and the prayerful reflection that must go with a mature Christian exercise of freedom.

THE PROBLEM WITH LAW

There is no doubt that Paul makes much of freedom. "It is for liberty that Christ freed us," he writes in Galatians 5.1.

He was writing against the background of his understanding of law. Law insists, "Do this! " or "Don't do that! " But it gives no power to live up to its "do's" and "don'ts."

A red traffic light signals that the driver of the car ought to stop. If he is distracted, or reckless, or asleep, or drunk, or simply going too fast, the signal will not slow down or halt the car. The law, "Stop for a red light," has no force to insure that it will be kept. The fear that a policeman may be parked around the corner may make the driver stop, but not the law itself.

A mother tells her four-year-old, "Don't go out into the street." Her words themselves, her law, will not prevent the child from racing into the street after a ball or to wave to a friend. The memory of swats he has received on the bottom for disregarding his mother's orders in the past may pull him up just before he steps onto the forbidden asphalt, but not the command itself.

Law is outside man. It can tell one what to do but it cannot overcome the obstacles in the way of keeping that law, no matter how good the law may be. We have already noted that laws against discrimination do not root out discrimination from hearts. Only the fear of punishment for disregarding the law brings about grudging acceptance of the rights of all.

The same holds true for the religious sphere. There are many religious laws. "Go to Mass on Sunday." "Thou shalt not steal." "Honor thy father and thy mother."

Human history has been marked by a disregard of laws, religious and civil, even those which seem sensible and good. The problem is that knowing something as good and being told to do it, and knowing something as evil and being told not to do it is simply not enough. Too many other considerations enter in. "I know I shouldn't steal — but if I take just this $100, I'll be able to afford something extra for a change." "I know I shouldn't spread this story about X, but Y, with whom I'm speaking, will think it's very funny." "I'd like to go to Mass, but I'm tired." And so it goes.

TRUE FREEDOM

A person comes closest to freedom when he recognizes the good in good laws and keeps them because of the value he accepts.

The man who stops for the red light is maturing in freedom if he has the good sense to realize the potential disaster in his shooting across the intersection. The four-year-old is moving toward freedom when he stops at the curb because he is aware of the dangers of being hit by a car.

Paul wants all to be free of law, of outside regulation, in order to live by a power that works within, the power, the "law" of love.

Love is different from all other laws because it is a force working inside man. Love is a sharing in the life of God himself that makes one care, act, forgive as the Father does.

The Christian must strive to be free of law but this does not mean that he can do whatever he wants. His freedom is freedom to love, to place himself at the service of God and others. How different this idea of freedom is from some of the distorted versions so popular today. True freedom is freedom to be as Jesus was, trusting in his Father, open to and caring for others.

FREEDOM AND LAW

If the goal is to become free of law, why are there religious laws? Why are there Ten Commandments? Why does the Church take moral stands? Why does the Church have standards of conduct that it expects its members to observe?
Why do we not exercise our freedom and decide the best way for us personally to live and love?

Laws are still needed, even among those who claim Jesus Christ has freed them.

We are too prone to self-deception, to the conviction that what is comfortable and agreeable is right. We need the community, guided by God, to point out directions, to act as a sounding board for what we may do as individuals.

"I don't believe that missing Mass on Sunday is a sin."
What better are you doing to deepen your sharing in the life of the Eucharistic Lord? Is your attitude to the law a real example of growing maturity and freedom, or is it a weak excuse for a lack of faith which makes Sunday Mass something of a chore?

"I don't believe pre-marital or extra-marital sex is wrong. I have been liberated from antiquated morality." Is that true?
Are you liberated? Or are you a slave to a kind of selfishness which uses persons like toys to provide recreation?

These few examples should make the point.

In the ideal, there should be no need for laws or regulations.
There should only be the force of love burning inside people and moving them to be noble and generous in every situation.

Unfortunately, sin is still around and while it is, it's just too easy for all of us to kid ourselves. Even the Church must have laws and regulations as a challenge to those who are part of it.

Those who would disregard those laws must ask themselves, "Why?" It may be that a regulation is out of date, no longer needed, perhaps even harmful to growth. If so, it should be changed or abolished or disregarded. It is also possible that the law still spells out a real value that every Christian should observe. If a person disregards the law, how else does he recognize the value?

The person growing in freedom observes the good law because he sees the value it is trying to preserve. The freest person of all needs no laws because love guides his whole life.

SUGGESTIONS FOR REFLECTION

1. Sometimes Catholics consider their own moral life and actions to be nobody else's business. If they do or do not attend Mass on Sunday, it's their own affair; whether or not they do acts of charity, or tell the truth at all times they consider their own concern. From his instruction about eating the meat from the temple sacrifices, how would Paul answer these persons?

2. Parents and teachers frequently use a principle that Paul endorses here. Describe an occasion when as a parent or teacher you freely gave up a right that was truly yours for the greater good of your children or students. Consider a time when you, as a husband or wife, did the same for your marriage partner.

3. Raising children in the Catholic religion is not easy. Give an example of how "meeting people where they are" may imply different practices for immature Christians than for mature Christians. How would this apply to adults who are still immature Christians?

4. Human example is a powerful force in society. Mention a time you saw it as an obstacle to the word being preached; as an aid to the word being preached.

5. It takes much inner freedom and prayer to distinguish a matter of principle from what is not, and to act accordingly in a dilemma. Give an example from your life when you resolved this tension. Were you at peace with the decision?

6. What might have been the historical outcome if Paul encouraged the women to go without veils and headdresses in his time?

7. Paul's emphasis was rather on Christians living out their relationship with Jesus than on changing the social structures of his time. Prepare a one-minute "spot" for radio to reconstruct what he might say to a particular Liberation Movement today (e. g., Women's, Black, Third World, etc.) working to reform the institutions of the world. Would the Liberationists agree with Paul?

8. Why would the changes decreed by Vatican Council II have received greater acceptance if more Catholics were familiar with Paul's idea of mature freedom with responsibility?

9. Adolescents naturally rebel against authority. How can they better be brought to respect and understand the law of freedom that Paul teaches?

10. Every day brings new decisions and actions to all of us. As you reflect back on today with its decisions and actions, try to identify your attitude toward freedom or law for the things you said or did. Was there a consistent pattern? Will any new insight from this chapter cause you to consider your reasons for action differently in the future?

CHAPTER V

THE LORD'S SUPPER

Please read: 1 Corinthians 11. 17-34

From the very beginning, Christians have come together to celebrate the Lord's Supper. What did the Eucharist mean to the Corinthians?

SUNDAY AT CORINTH

Various hints suggest that the liturgy as celebrated at Corinth in the 50's might have gone something like this.

The Christians, mostly of the poorer and slave classes, met on Sunday in the home of a member of the community. Their meeting lasted for a good part of the day, probably through the afternoon and into the evening. The sessions were rather free-wheeling. One person might offer aloud a spontaneous prayer; another chant a hymn that appealed to him. Still another might prophesy, that is, give a sermon encouraging to a deeper Christian life. Yet another might speak in tongues, which we will consider later. There would also be teaching to provide further insight into the meaning of the Christian faith and its implications for everyday living.

This part of the service was apparently so loosely structured that several of these activities might be going on at the same time, giving rise to a lively, if noisy, experience. Not unlike modern Catholics, the Corinthians were arriving all through this session.

One regular feature of the lengthy gathering seems to have been the opportunity to eat a meal. Each family or group brought its own lunch basket and the variety and quantity of the menu depended on the resources of the family. At some point, the actual Lord's Supper was celebrated.

This liturgy differed from the more formal liturgy of the Jewish synagogue. There, the framework of the service consisted of opening prayer, reading from the Hebrew Scriptures, comment on the reading, final prayer.

THE CELEBRATION OF THE LORD'S SUPPER

Paul comes to the actual Eucharist in verses 23-25. "I received from the Lord what I handed on to you, namely, that the Lord Jesus on the night in which he was betrayed took bread, and after he had given thanks, broke it and said, 'This is my body, which is for you. Do this in remembrance of me.' In the same way, after the supper, he took the cup, saying, 'This cup is the new covenant in my blood. Do this, whenever you drink it, in remembrance of me.' "

In this account of the Eucharist as it was being celebrated by the church at Corinth, Paul provides the oldest written description of the Eucharistic ritual.

Where did this rite of celebrating come from?

The answer, "It comes from what Jesus did at the Last Supper," is both correct and too simple.

The four accounts of the words of the first Eucharist — Matthew 26.26-28; Mark 14.22-24; Luke 22.19-20; 1 Corinthians 11.24-26 — do not all say the same thing in the same way. Moreover Paul was not at the Last Supper. Where did he get his version?

Paul says, "I received . . . what I handed on." In the language of the rabbis Paul is saying that he taught the Corinthians what he himself had been taught about the Lord's Supper. He was the bridge that carried the ritual and meaning of the Eucharist to the Corinthians, not in 57 when he wrote this letter, but in 50 or 51 when he first visited Corinth.

Where did the other end of the bridge touch down? Where was the tradition coming *from?*

Without going into details, we might observe that there are indications that Paul had gotten his version of the Eucharist from the church at Antioch when he lived there in the early 40's.

In other words, Paul reminds the Corinthians of what they already believed about the Eucharist. That understanding of the Eucharist was not Paul's invention but was part of the traditional instruction of the Church that had been imparted to Paul in his early years as a Christian. That instruction on the Eucharist must be kept in mind now in the particular situation in which the Corinthians find themselves.

THE LORD'S SUPPER AS A SACRIFICE

Jesus' body and Jesus' blood mean that the total person of Jesus is present. The division into body and blood recalls the separation of blood from body that took place when the animal victims were sacrificed as recounted in the Old Testament.

People need some way to express what they feel and believe. Life is full of signs and symbols — a bottle of perfume on Mother's Day, a necktie on a birthday, a family dinner on an anniversary. The emotions that arise inside need some outlet.

Religion shares in this universal human yearning. People need to express in some gesture what they feel toward that power which they believe to rule life. This is true no mat-

ter how they look on that power, as good or evil, as loving
or tyrannical.

The sacrifice of the Israelites made visible and tangible their
relationship to Yahweh. In a sacrifice, a gift was first offered
to God, then destroyed totally or partially. The gift might
vary from a small basket of grain to a sheep or an ox.

The killing or destruction by fire showed the permanence
of the offering. There could be no taking back of what
had been given. It also placed the gift in the invisible do-
main where God lived.

The ceremony could concretize a number of interior sentiments of the offerer: praise to God for what he is —
the creator and helper of men; thanks to God for some
specific favor he had granted, a good harvest, for example;
repentance for having offended God by sin.

THE DANGER IN RITUAL

In any situation where signs and symbols are used, the problem for integrity is to have the interior feeling match the
gesture. You may give a gift to a friend, not out of esteem
but because that person has influence you would like to
tap into later. I may shake hands, and detest the one whose
hand I'm holding.

Religion faces the same problem. The outward gesture can
be a lie when the inner feeling that it is supposed to be
expressing just isn't there, not even in the desire.

This danger in ritual is nothing new. The Israelite prophets
were strong in their denunciation of religion that was merely the outer shell of sacrifice and wordy prayers, empty of
real closeness to God.

JESUS' DEATH AS SINCERE SACRIFICE

Certain moments in a life sum up what that life has been.

A wealthy man leaves $1,000,000 to a charitable cause. Those in the know say that this is just the high point of the man's lifelong work for that cause.

A policeman is killed trying to rescue a child from a burning building. His friends say that this was an indication of the dedication to helping others that had been the chief characteristic of his whole life.

When Jesus died on the cross, that moment caught perfectly what his life had been all along.

In the words of the Eucharist that Paul uses, a dimension of Jesus' life that is especially clear is his taking up of the role of the Servant of God. The Servant of God is a mysterious personage who appears in some passages of the Book of Isaiah (42.1-4; 49.1-6; 50.4-9; 52.13-52.12). The Servant, according to these passages, is chosen by God to bring his message to the world. The Servant meets rejection, persecution and ultimately death. By his death, even though he is innocent of any guilt, he saves his people from sin.

Whoever this Servant might have been in the period when these passages were written — over 500 years before the birth of Jesus — the early Christians saw them as a remarkable prophecy of Jesus.

Jesus especially showed his love and obedience to his Father and his love for his fellow men through his fidelity to his role as Servant, the one who brought God's message to men even in the face of suffering and a horrible death. Jesus offered his whole life to his Father's work. The interior truth of that offering was demonstrated in the act of accepting death on the cross. Jesus' death is the sacrifice where the love and obedience that make up man's true relationship with God find perfect expression.

THE LORD'S SUPPER AS A SYMBOL OF ONENESS

Among the ancient people of the Bible, sharing a meal meant sharing life. To feed a guest was to take on a special relationship to him, to assume responsibility for him.

Even today, sharing a meal often communicates some sense of belonging. Family meals on special occasions like a marriage or baptism show and strengthen family unity. Social and benevolent societies make dinners or banquets important. Lions or Kiwanians or Knights of Columbus or volunteer firemen come together for more than the roast beef dinner.

The meal they share indicates that they also share the goals and aspirations of the group to which they belong.

To share a meal in a religious context was to deepen the relationship with God who was being honored and with the others who shared the meal. The very fact that Jesus asked his disciples to eat a meal with him and that his disciples continued to come together for meals after his death indicates a sharing in his life and with one another.

The final union of God and his people in the reign of universal and lasting peace was also symbolized by a meal.
"On this mountain the Lord of hosts will provide for all peoples
A feast of rich food and choice wines, juicy, rich food and pure choice wines.
On this mountain he will destroy the veil that veils all peoples,
The web that is woven over all nations; he will destroy death forever" (Is 25.6-8).

This idea is the background for the Gospel passages where Jesus describes the kingdom of God as a banquet or feast.

The Eucharistic meal unites God to men and men with men in an imperfect yet real way now. The fact that people of all times and all nations and all backgrounds share that meal is a beginning of the perfect and complete unity that God will one day bring.

THE LORD'S SUPPER AND PASSOVER

The main feature of the Passover was the Passover or Paschal lamb. The lamb was killed, roasted and eaten according to carefully detailed rules. The full meaning of the Passover can be left to the study of the Old Testament. Here, it is sufficient to notice that the Passover was a symbol of liberation. The Israelites had been slaves in Egypt. God had delivered them from that slavery. The ritual of the lamb commemorated that liberation.

However, celebrating the Passover was not just a glance backward to what had happened many centuries before. It was a symbolic way of making present that same liberating power of God that had burst forth in the past. Enemies there would always be: people, events, circumstances that prevented the Israelites from being truly free. Sometimes conquerors from foreign lands crushed their freedom. Sometimes their own sinfulness and confusion enslaved them and pulled them far from God.

Whatever kept God's people from him was a slavemaster and only God himself could free his people. This freeing power was especially active in the celebration of the Passover.

One day there would be a final, complete and lasting liberation. This the Passover also celebrated.

Whether or not the Last Supper that Jesus celebrated was the actual Jewish Passover meal of the year that he died is still a matter of discussion by scholars. Whatever the historical situation, the Gospels speak of the Last Supper in terms which connect it to the Passover. Knowing what the Passover was about helps to understand what the Last Supper was about.

Jesus is to be seen in terms of Passover. The Passover celebrated the liberation from Egypt. Jesus' death was the ultimate liberation for man, the liberation from Sin and Death.

To face the example of Jesus' life and death; to receive from him the strength to live according to that example; to begin now to enter into that life with the hope of complete union with him one day — all this comes through the celebration of the Eucharist.

Just as the Passover meal was not a ceremonial looking only to the past but a channel into the present for God's power, the celebration of the Eucharist is not simply a commemoration of what Jesus did in the past. To celebrate the Lord's Supper is to be brought into personal contact with Jesus and his saving power.

THE LORD'S SUPPER AND THE NEW COVENANT

The Israelites were aware that they stood in a special relationship with God. When they tried to put into words more exactly what this relationship was, they found that an institution familiar to them, the covenant, expressed it rather well. A covenant was an agreement in which a more powerful king laid certain demands — loyalty, help in war, taxes — on a lesser king and in turn promised to watch over his interests, to help him, to protect him.

The simple formula in which the Israelites eventually came to express the terms of the covenant or agreement between God and them was: "I will be your God and you will be my people." God would be their loving protector and liberator. They, in turn, must recognize him alone as the core of their existence and live out this recognition in the quality of their lives.

Exodus 24 describes a ritual whereby the covenant between God and the Israelites was ratified. Young bulls were killed.

Their blood, the sign of life, was collected. Some was splashed on an altar, the symbol of God. 'The rest was sprinkled over the people. The same blood designating life, touched both God, represented by the altar, and his people. The "blood of the covenant" joined God to his people by a bond of life.

The history recorded in the Old Testament is a chronicle of the great difficulty the Israelites had in living up to their part of the covenant. They were continuously pulled aside to worship other gods, to adopt ways of life incompatible with their belief in Yahweh.

In fact, the judgment of some prophets is that the Israelites were so caught up in a tragic pattern of sin and infidelity that it was humanly impossible for them ever to return to God and be faithful to him.

"Can the Ethiopian change his skin? the leopard his spots? As easily would you be able to do good,
    accustomed to evil as you are" (Jer 13.23).

Instead of falling into despair, prophets began to talk of a new covenant.

Jeremiah proclaims: "The days are coming, says the LORD, when I will make a new covenant with the house of Israel and the house of Judah. It will not be like the covenant I made with their fathers the day I took them by the hand to lead them forth from the land of Egypt; for they broke my covenant, and I had to show myself their master, says the LORD. But this is the covenant which I will make with the house of Israel after those days, says the LORD. I will place my law within them, and write it upon their hearts; I will be their God, and they shall by my people. No longer will they have need to teach their friends and kinsmen how to know the LORD. All, from least to greatest, shall know me, says the LORD, for I will forgive their evildoing and remember their sin no more" (31.31-34).

Jeremiah holds forth hope for a radical change that will transform man because of what God does. Man could not keep his part of the covenant with God. He was mired in sin. There was a weakness in man that spread until it operpowered him.

But instead of rejecting human beings once and for all, God would make a new covenant, establish a new relationship with them. The difference betweeen this relationship and the old one that had failed would be that instead of just showing people how to live, God would place in them a new power, a new "heart" that would enable them to live as God's own.

This is the meaning of "the new covenant in my blood" in the words of the Eucharist. The Lord's Supper and the death of Jesus are part of this new relationship between God and his people. The life and death of Jesus spill forth into man a flood of new life which opens up the possibility of life as true sons of God. The Lord's Supper makes available to all the very life of Jesus himself.

Instead of the blood of animals sprinkled over people and altar to effect a bond between man and God, the death of Jesus re-presented in the celebration of the Eucharist joins man to God in the most intimate bond possible, the bond of common life.

THE LORD'S SUPPER "IN REMEMBRANCE OF ME"

Christians come together to celebrate the Eucharist in response to Jesus' command, "Do this in remembrance of me."

Remembrance is not simply a wistful look backward, as the remembrance of the Fourth of July might be, or the remembrance stirred by snapshots of a long past and very pleasant vacation. Remembrance at the Eucharist brings into the here and now what Jesus did, his offering of himself in love and obedience to the Father. The Eucharist makes present that peak moment of self-giving on the cross so that Christians of every age might join in that offering and might receive from Jesus the strength to live it out.

THE LORD'S SUPPER, "PROCLAIMING THE DEATH OF THE LORD UNTIL HE COMES"

The "coming of the Lord" is something to look forward to with hope and eagerness. The coming of the Lord means perfect and everlasting peace, unity and love.

The Lord's Supper "makes" the Lord come. In the Eucharistic celebration is to be found the strength for peace, unity and love flowing from the death of Jesus on the cross. As Christians grow in these qualities, they make the presence of the Lord more evident. The Eucharist, by its transforming effect on those who share in it with faith, actually makes the coming of the Lord "nearer."

THE LORD'S SUPPER AND THE LIFE OF THE COMMUNITY

Paul has introduced the theology of the Eucharist into his correspondence with the Corinthians not because he wishes to give a lesson for its own sake. He faces a problem in the life of the community.

At the meal during the Sunday gathering of Christians, things have gotten mixed up. "Everyone is in haste to eat his own supper. One person goes hungry while another gets drunk. Do you not have homes where you can eat and drink? "

Groups of family or friends brought their own lunches and wine to the Christian assembly. Some were evidently drinking too much and turning the gathering into a party. Others had plenty of food for themselves and ate their fill, while members of the community who were poor and could not afford to bring food could only look on while hunger pains gnawed.

Paul insists that as long as this was happening, the Christians at Corinth misunderstood the Lord's Supper.

The Lord's Supper is supposed to deepen in those who share in it the life of Jesus. The characteristic of Jesus' life was his giving. He gave even his life for those who needed him. How could the Corinthians eat the Lord's Supper and mock the giving of Jesus by ignoring the hungry sitting in the same room?

The Lord's Supper is supposed to heighten the unity that exists among those who share it. How can the Christians eat the Lord's Supper and be so unconcerned over the plight of their brothers and sisters?

Paul writes strong words: "He who eats and drinks without recognizing the body eats and drinks a judgment on himself."

The problem the Corinthians must face is not doubt about the "real presence," i. e., that Jesus is truly among them in the celebration of the Eucharist. Their fault is that they are failing to live up to the social demands involved in growing in the life of Jesus. They do not recognize the body of the community, the unity and mutual concern that should go with being Christian. They have failed to follow the example of Jesus who lived and died "for you" and are living only for themselves.

THE LORD'S SUPPER TODAY

The depth and richness of the Eucharist has not changed. We might let Paul challenge our own understanding of and attitude to the Eucharist by summing up the main points taught in 1 Corinthians 11.17-34.

1. The Eucharist is Jesus' sacrifice, made in love and obedience to the Father.

2. The Lord's Supper is a meal which deepens the union between man and God and among men.

3. The Lord's Supper deepens our union with Jesus, the freest of all men. He was free of any concern less than loving and serving his Father and loving men. He becomes the great liberating force for us.

4. The Lord's Supper does not simply remind us of what Jesus did. It makes Jesus present for us in the act of offering himself so that we might join ourselves with him and then receive the strength to live out this union.

5. Participation in the Lord's Supper involves community. To share the Eucharist with integrity means to become more mature in the life of Jesus, and more aware of the needs of our brothers.

6. The Lord's Supper is not magic. Reception of the Eucharist will not change us automatically. In the Eucharist we do not receive a pill or a medicine. We meet a Person. As with any other personal encounter, something happens only when we are open to hear and to see. We must be open to hear the challenge that Jesus presents and to accept from him the power to be more like him.

7. The Lord's Supper points to what God plans. A common faith in the presence of Jesus in the Eucharist manages, at least during the time of the Eucharistic celebration, to tear down the various barriers that separate races, social classes, age groups. This is an indication of what will be when the full and final presence of Jesus will tear aside forever all barriers that separate people and bring in his never-ending rule of peace and love.

SUGGESTIONS FOR REFLECTION

1. What is a "sacrifice"? Some parents do not use this word in their homes today because they think it an old-fash-

ioned concept. Do you find this concept commonly app-
reciated among your neighbors, business associates, family?
In speaking of the Mass we emphasize the meal or banquet
as well as the sacrifice. Which has more meaning for your
life as you think of the Mass?

2. The world of advertising has blown up gift-giving at Christmas, Mother's Day, etc. How can the idea of "sacrifice" as
gift-giving of self in order to thank, to ask forgiveness, to
appreciate, be brought more effectively into the sentiments
of all of us: children, adolescents, adults?

3. Describe or draw a meal or banquet that stands out in
your memory because it deepened relationships and brought
greater unity among the guests. Why is such a banquet a foretaste of heaven?

4. Realistically, can unity and concern of all men for all
men as brothers symbolized by the Eucharistic banquet,
ever be achieved? Who or why not? Is the "Sign of Peace"
at Mass a step in this direction?

5. The Eucharist unites us in the death and resurrection
of Jesus now. Mention one occasion of dying and rising to
new life you can personally remember; i. e., moving from
a familiar neighborhood as dying; making new friends in
the new neighborhood as rising, etc.

6. Do you believe you can earn salvation by being good in
life? Review the new covenant prophesy of Jeremiah (31:
31-34) and reflect on what he says of our personal ability to
reach union with God. If God is always the initiator and ex-
tender in the relationship, what radical attitude is necessary
for us to keep the covenant?

7. "The proof of the Sunday Mass fellowship is after Mass
in the parking lot," said one parishioner. The Eucharist
should have a "transforming effect on those who share in
it," helping them become less selfish and more self-giving.

Is this the experience of your family, friends, business associates? How could it become more so? What attitudes would it require of all who participate, before, during, and after?

8. In America we see competition as a virtue and claim that success comes with hard work. We praise the "go-getter." How can the Eucharist make us more conscious of giving, of mutual concern, of cooperation, of re-enacting personally, "This is my body which is given for you"? What would this mean for the business world, sports, child psychology, leadership training?

CHAPTER VI

HOW A COMMUNITY OF CHRISTIANS SHOULD LIVE

People are funny. There's nothing so good that we can't use it for the wrong purpose. There's no cause so noble that we can't pervert it. There's no feeling so sacred that we can't distort it.

A close look at oneself can be a scary experience. Try to determine with certainty why you do this rather than that. Can you be sure of the motivation for even the best things you've done?

Am I patient with other people because I respect them or simply because it takes ten tons of dynamite to make me react to anything? Did I help that person who needed help because I cared or because I wanted other people to notice how good I am?

Asking questions like these makes for deep digging and we can't always be sure how objective and honest our answers will be.

Because we are such unpredictable creatures, so prone to twisting life to suit our own purposes, an absolute need for all of us is the ability to discern — to make responsible judgments about whether we are acting to serve God and others or ourselves.

The Corinthians were involved in a situation which required

clear thinking and a precise awareness of Christian values. As usual, Paul took a hand to set the Corinthians on the way to being able to see correctly.

WHAT WAS HAPPENING AT CORINTH

Please read: 1 Corinthians 12-14

In our own time, the possibility of humans being taken over by the devil has attracted much attention. The person possessed acts in strange and frightening ways. An evil personality seems to take over the body and use it for its own vicious and obscene purposes.

The ancient world was just as interested in the possibility of a person being taken over by a god. Such a person could do remarkable things, like foretelling the future, or speaking in strange languages. The person actually seemed to lose contact with what he had been. The state of such a person was called ecstasy, which meant being possessed by a divine power.

Whatever the explanation, the people at Corinth were familiar with such phenomena. They knew of prophetesses and prophets at shrines of the gods, who answered questions about the future while in a trance. They knew of pagan religious ceremonies in which devotees seemed to be lifted into another world and spoke mysterious, unintelligible words.

These contacts had their effect on the attitudes of those Corinthians who had become Christians.

The Corinthians had learned well the lesson that all Christians are indeed "taken over" in a certain sense by God. The Spirit, the life of God himself, dwells in those who believe in him and in the community which professes its faith in him.

What was confusing the Corinthians was how the presence

of the Spirit could be seen and recognized. Through what human actions does God reveal himself?

The Christians at Corinth were caught up in a bizarre competition, trying to outdo one another in showing who had "more" of the Spirit. They had established the right rule — you should be able to tell a Christian by the signs of God's life in his behavior. They had misread what the signs of God's life are.

CHARISMS – GIFTS OF THE SPIRIT

In his history of loving care for men, God has shared his life with men so that they might carry on his saving work.

In the Old Testament, God gave his power to men like Moses and Joshua so that they could lead his people. He had given his spirit to prophets so that they could correct the faults of his people and direct them back to God. What would make the ideal Israelite king was God's spirit which would enable the king to rule with wisdom and justice.

These special qualities are called "charisms," special powers that God gives to some people to use for the benefit of others in carrying out his loving design for mankind.

God continued — and continues — to work in the same way after the coming of Jesus. He endows some people with a special sharing in his life so that they can lead other men to truth and life.

It would be a mistake to consider these charisms as always, or even most of the time, out of the ordinary.

Paul gives a list of charisms in 1 Corinthians 12.8-10 and 12.28-30. Some seem on the spectacular side: "the gift of healing," "miraculous powers."

Others are part of the ordinary working of the community.

73

"Prophecy" is a gift for encouraging and exhorting the community by saying the right things at the right time. "Teaching" is the ability to put before the community the further implications for belief and conduct once the basic commitment to Jesus has been made.

THE GIFT OF TONGUES

One manifestation of the presence of the Spirit which especially fascinated the Corinthians was called "tongues" or "glossolalia."

Unfortunately, it is very difficult to know precisely what happened when someone spoke in tongues.

The impression given by the Pentecost story in Acts 2 is that speaking in tongues was an ability to be understood by people whose language was foreign to the speaker. Everyone in the crowd at Jerusalem, gathered from all parts of the world, is said to have understood the apostles as "speaking in his own language."

In 1 Corinthians, however, it is presumed that the words spoken by the person with the gift are not understood by those who hear and so need an interpreter.

Scholars offer a number of possibilities for what "tongues" means here.

1. As in Acts 2, "tongues" means speaking in a real language. However, the language spoken is unknown to the speaker and often to the hearer. This might happen if, for example, a person whose language is English, speaking to others who also use English, without any training or preparation suddenly broke into Hebrew.

2. "Tongues" is meaningless sounds in no language.

3. "Tongues" begins as intelligent speech praising God. As

the speaker's mood deepens and his religious experience takes hold, he slides into broken, unconnected sentences. These he intersperses with words in foreign languages, probably words learned from the liturgy — much as modern Catholics learned Hebrew words, "Hosanna," "Hallelujah," or Greek, "Kyrie, eleison," from the liturgy.

4. Some recent investigators of the phenomenon of "tongues" have called it "pre-conceptual prayer." They rule out foreign languages or even ecstasy. "Tongues" is sounds uttered as personal prayer. As a person contemplates God and perceives him with growing clarity, a reaction takes place. The person tries to express his faith and emotions. But words fail, so the best he can do is utter sounds which are not yet rational language.

A parallel might help. Suppose I am trying to remember the name of a person I knew many years ago. I have the picture of the person before my eyes. I can even hear in imagination the sound of his voice. But the name escapes me. I experience frustration that I am not able to recall the name. Instead of simply sitting quietly, I make a sound, perhaps a drawn-out "Mmmmmm." From the tone of voice, the inflection, someone listening could get a general idea of my impatience and frustration even though I have not expressed it in words that make sense.

Whatever happened when someone spoke in "tongues," clearly it was unusual — more striking than preaching a sermon, or teaching. And because it was unusual, the Corinthians found it attractive, something which was an impressive sign that the Spirit was working in a person, something which gave a person status in the community as one favored by God. Everybody wanted to be able to do it.

Because of this, God's gifts which were supposed to bring the community together, were dividing it. The community at Corinth was being split into groups on the basis of the various signs of having God's Spirit. The elite faction was the one made up of those able to speak in "tongues."

But could anything which was causing division possibly be a gift from God? What was needed was a good dose of discernment, of the ability to analyze carefully from God's standpoint what was going on so as to determine if it was really the work of God or the work of forces opposed to him.

Paul does not hesitate to take up the challenge.

THE FIRST RULE: ALL CHRISTIANS HAVE THE SPIRIT

Whereas the Corinthians set up their own rules to determine those in whom God's Spirit is working, Paul says that anyone who confesses with integrity the basic creed, "Jesus is Lord," has God's Spirit within.

While granting that the Spirit makes his presence felt differently in different believers, giving some a more sensitive appreciation of proper conduct, others an extraordinary faith, still others the power to heal, etc., Paul emphasizes that it is still the same Spirit manifesting his presence in all these ways.

THE BODY OF CHRIST

Paul then moves to a notion whose development is a particular contribution of his to Christian thought — the Church as the Body of Christ.

Most of the western world until recent times accepted an idea of the body strongly influenced by Greek philosophy. The body is something of a nuisance. It imprisons the soul. The soul is that wonderful, interior reality that lives forever, that is able to know, to will, to think, to love. But since that soul is trapped in an all-too-weak, limited and perishable body, it can never reach its full potential until it is freed from the body. When the body dies, the soul is liberated to begin a new life unhampered by the literally dead weight of the body.

With this state of mind, there is no great compliment in speaking of the Church as the "body of Christ." In this context of ideas, the Church would be a hindrance impeding Christ from what he might be.

But among people of a Semitic background, the attitude to the body was different. Body and soul are not two separate and isolated realities, the one trapped "inside" the other. Body and soul make one living person. The body is what gives the self the possibility of expressing itself. Through the body, a person comes in contact with the surrounding world. Through the body, the self makes its presence felt. Body and soul are needed for the self to be complete, whole, real.

When Jesus walked the dusty paths of Galilee and Judea, he laid his truth, his mercy, his compassion, his forgiveness, his challenge, before others through the words he spoke, through his gestures, through the emotions that showed in his face, through his touch. His body revealed what his deepest self was.

When Paul refers to the Church as the Body of Christ, he attributes to the community of Christians the same role that Jesus' physical body played in his lifetime. Jesus' love, truth, mercy, compassion, forgiveness, challenge become visible to the world in the life of the community of Christians.

Herein lies the challenge to Christians. They are to make their relations with one another and with the world the vibrant reflection of the life of Jesus himself. This awesome call can begin to be possible only because the same Spirit which is Jesus' life is also present in the Church.

Put bluntly, Jesus will be alive or dead within a given place to the extent that the Christian community there bears in itself the authentic life of Jesus and demonstrates this by the Jesus-like quality of its existence.

But even in his own lifetime, Jesus was misunderstood because of his own very real humanity. Many wondered how the one they called the "carpenter's son" could be God's chosen. He showed all the marks of humanity except for sin. He even died on the cross.

So also the community, the parish, the diocese, will be a human and imperfect reflection of the life of Jesus. Many will find it difficult to see Jesus behind the humanity and sinfulness of the community. The Christian vocation must be to make the reality of Jesus as credible as possible in the complex, day-by-day life of believers, as individuals and as a group. The great failure would be the Christian community which is so tainted by sin that no one could ever be expected to find Jesus dwelling within it.

Paul carries the body idea one step further. The body is made up of many different parts. Each part makes its own contribution to the total well-being of the body. Can you really compare an eye with an ear? Which is more important to have? Can you make a choice between an arm and a leg? Each is different from the other. Each is extremely important to the body. It would be a hard choice to decide which of the two we would be more willing to do without.

The body needs all its parts to function well, although each of these parts performs a different service.

The Christian community, the Church, needs different people with different gifts given by the Spirit. The church witnesses to the living presence of Jesus by the harmonious working of all its members in service of God's loving design.

SEX, FREEDOM AND THE BODY OF CHRIST
Please read: 1 Corinthians 6. 12-20

This passage is taken out of place and introduced here because it brings together the question of freedom considered previously, the theology of the Body of Christ, and the ever-important issue of sexual morality.

Some Corinthians — Christians — prided themselves on possessing a special kind of insight and knowledge that put them above the ordinary herd. They felt not bound by the morality that might hold others. For them, "Everything is lawful."

This applied also in the area of sexual conduct. They claimed that the use of sex is as natural as eating. Therefore they were free to follow their sexual inclinations with whomever they wished. (Strange how the more things change, the more they stay the same).

Paul shows this line of reasoning for what it is — an appalling contempt for the human body. The whole human person, including the body, makes up part of the presence of Jesus Christ in the world, is "a member of Christ." Jesus Christ himself is united to each Christian. When that Christian unites himself with an illicit sex partner, he defiles his union with Jesus. He sins against himself because he separates himself from his relationship with Christ. He sins against Christ because his conduct makes him a monstrous and grotesque carrier of the presence of Christ.

WHO CONTRIBUTES MOST?

Paul's first and major point has been to emphasize that every Christian in the community, if God's life is truly in him, makes his own unique and indispensable contribution to making the community a more believable sign of Jesus' presence. The local church needs all the special individual qualities that each member brings. There should be no competition among Christians about who is more important.

Having said this, Paul comes in chapter 13 to the greatest power of all — LOVE.

There's that word that has fallen into such disrepute today.

It has been used to justify some of the most outlandish conduct. It has been applied with equal seriousness to two adolescents gazing soulfully into each other's eyes and panting heavily and to a couple that has faced life together for fifty years of marriage. It has been pressed into service as a synonym for sex, for lust, for irresponsibility, for selfishness.

There is no confusion, no uncertainty about the meaning of love for Paul. He describes in detail what love is all about.

"Love is patient; love is kind. Love is not jealous, it does not put on airs, it is not snobbish. Love is never rude, it is not self-seeking, it is not prone to anger; neither does it brood over injuries. Love does not rejoice in what is wrong but rejoices with the truth. There is no limit to love's forbearance, to its trust, its hope, its power to endure."

Patience is the strength to endure injury without trying for revenge and without display of temper.

Kindness is generosity, eagerness to be of service to others.

The *jealousy love avoids* is quarrelsome bickering, such as that in which the Corinthians were indulging by forming their cliques.

Putting on airs is incompatible with love because it involves the loss of a sense of proportion. Some Corinthians were losing sight of what was important by insisting on their "freedom" to the harm of others, or by exaggerating the prestige of talking in tongues.

Love *excludes snobbishness,* which is an overblown sense of one's own importance and talents.

Love *rules out rudeness,* the lack of tact and consideration. Under this heading, it would never tolerate the unbecoming eating and drinking during the Sunday assembly at Corinth.

Love *does not allow self-seeking,* the insistence on one's own rights and privileges, the focusing on one's own self.

Love *does not brood over injuries,* but holds off from judging the wrong it believes it finds in a neighbor and forgets the evil it has endured. Love rejoices when truth and justice prevail and is willing to recognize and praise goodness in others, unlike the Corinthians who were stingy in admitting and being thankful for the gifts of the Spirit in their brothers.

Love is ready to make allowances; to excuse; to trust others and not suspect their motives and actions; to hope for good in others even when disappointed; not to be crushed even when it is met with coldness, ingratitude, and insult.

Love is unique because it is the foretaste of life with God. All the charisms or gifts are intended to bring man to God. In God's presence, they all become unnecessary and pass from existence. The one experience that continues from this life into life with God is love which is the essence of God's life.

Paul ends his description of love with the logical conclusion — "There are in the end three things that last: faith, hope, and love, and the greatest of these is love. Seek eagerly after love."

FIRST THINGS FIRST IN CHARISMS

After his praise of Christian love, Paul returns to a general rule. "Since you have set your hearts on spiritual gifts, try to be rich in those that build up the church" (14.12).

The purpose of the charisms, the spiritual gifts, is to make the community a sign of Jesus' presence. Belonging to the community should deepen the faith, the hope, the love, of all who are members. The life of the community should draw those who are not yet believers. The life of the community should have the attractiveness of Jesus himself.

Those gifts count for most which contribute most to this result. The preacher who moves the community to perform an obvious act of care for another. The teacher who helps the community see more clearly what Jesus is all about and begin to live according to this deeper insight. The administrator who provides for the orderly operation of community affairs and gives its members a sense of peace and security. The apostle who brings the basic call of Jesus in its appeal and challenge. These are all moved by the Spirit, share his gifts and contribute to the maturing of the community.

So also does the person with the gift of healing. Or the one who speaks in "tongues."

There is no need to organize these into a hierarchy in which one is better than another. If anyone should be foolish enough for that kind of game-playing, that gift of the Spirit is not best which attracts the most attention (as, for example, an exorcist might in our peculiar times), but that which does most to make the life of the community look more like the life of Jesus Christ.

THE CHURCH TODAY

From what Paul has written in chapters 12-14, we can reflect on the experience of the Church today.

1. God moves in creating a new world free from sin through the lives and activities of men and women. Most of these lives and activities will seem very ordinary. But biblical history, the self-revelation of God, shows that that is his way. We ought not expect a universe full of miraculous and spectacular occurrences with neon lights advertising God.

2. God can live and work in all those who believe in him. God gives his own life to human beings, just as parents share their life with their child. This sharing of human life begins in conception and continues while the child is at home. When all is working properly, the child grows in being human through the knowledge, values, ideals, attitudes his parents communicate and share with him. The sharing of God's life begins with Baptism and matures through a constant, living relationship with him.

3. God lives not only in Christians as individuals, but also in the Christian community. The community of those who have accepted God as revealed by Jesus make up the "Body of Christ," the contemporary presence of Jesus in the world. Through the Church, his Body today, Jesus reaches out and touches our society.

4. Every parish community, every Christian grouping, has as its chief reason for existence to make visible in its own area of operation the love, the mercy, the compassion, the challenge to a deeper and truer life manifested by Jesus. This happens when, in spite of its diversity, in spite of conflicts and disagreements which are bound to arise, the most obvious characteristic of the community is love. The community fails when it is so torn apart, so petty, so concerned about things that don't count, that it blots out any signs of Jesus' presence.

5. Love is not a blob of silly-putty that can be worked into any shape that suits our purposes. Paul, and the Christian tradition, are very definite about what love means.

6. The only competition that should exist among Christians is the never-ceasing effort to reveal more of Jesus' life. The great strength of any Christian group is that what one person lacks in himself, the community provides. Each member can contribute by his own talents and qualities to the over-all image the community portrays of the richness and goodness of the life of Jesus.

7. The parish, the Church, is never all that it should be. It never becomes an absolutely clear sign of Jesus' presence because it never puts off its own humanity and sinfulness. It can never stop growing and developing. The motto is, "Build up the Body," i. e., make the community an ever more vital, an ever more impressive sign of Jesus alive in the world.

SUGGESTIONS FOR REFLECTION

1. The Corinthians knew the right rule, "You should be able to tell a Christian by the signs of God's life in his behavior," but they had misread what the signs of God's life are. What are the signs of God's life (holiness) that today's Americans look for in a person's behavior? How do they compare with those signs the Corinthians respected? How do they fit with Paul's "signs of God's life"?

2. Is the gift of tongues as a charism a cause of division in today's Church?

3. How can we tell whether or not certain gifts are the work of God or of forces opposed to him?

4. The Greek idea of man was: body and soul at war in the human person. The Semitic idea of man was: body revealing the total personality or self. Which approach do you favor? How would a person's approach affect his idea of life and death? Which is Paul's idea when he speaks of the community as the Body of Christ? Can the Body of Christ exhibit imperfections of humanity and still be true?

5. What are your particular gifts or charisms for the Body of Christ today? Are you free to use them in service? Have you considered using them in teaching, being a lector, as a minister to the sick, etc.?

6. Parents today complaim of the religion program, "All we ever hear is love, love, love. That's all they teach the chil-

dren. The basics seem forgotten! " In view of Paul's song of praise of love as the greatest gift, how would you respond to the complaint? Could a child or teen-ager understand the meaning of love as Paul describes it?

7. The love in your parish community should be an attracting sign of Jesus' presence for the members and for those outside. Is this true of your parish community? Where do you personally find that kind of love present today? How do you personally stand with regard to the characteristics of love that Paul mentions?

8. What is grace? Is paragraph No. 3 on page 73 speaking of grace as you have described it?

9. Have you ever shared life with anyone? Were you a giver or a receiver of life? Describe the occasion and why you consider it such. Then try to explain how God shares his life with human beings. As a receiver in this sharing relationship, what kind of response do you make? How?

10. Obviously we do not have a perfect, "absolutely clear sign of Jesus' presence" in any community of human beings, including the Church. Is this good or bad? Helpful or a hindrance to growth and development?

CHAPTER VII

THE RESURRECTION: JESUS' AND OURS

Please read: 1 Corinthians 15

"Tell me, if Christ is preached as raised from the dead, how is it that some of you say there is no resurrection of the dead? If there is no resurrection of the dead, Christ himself has not be raised. And if Christ has not been raised, our preaching is void of content and your faith is empty too."

So writes Paul to the Christians at Corinth.

What made these affirmations and the lengthy arguments and explanations of Chapter 15 necessary?

LIFE AFTER DEATH: DREAM OR REALITY?

The fact of death raises many questions — questions which are not just intellectual fun and games but determine one's stance toward life.

Is death the End, or does life continue even after the clods of earth have covered the coffin?

If there is life after death, what is that life like?

If there is life after death, how does one plug into it?

If there is life after death, what happens to the body which obviously corrupts into skeleton and then dust?

DEATH AMONG THE PAGANS

The non-Jewish world influenced by Greek and Roman culture offered a wide variety of beliefs in what happened once death came.

The great Roman *poet,* Virgil (70-19 B.C.) paints an imaginative picture of the underworld. A boatman, Charon, waits to ferry the souls of the dead across the river Styx into Hades. A howling, three-headed dog, Cerberus, guards the entrance to the underworld. Once inside, the wicked are tormented for their evil deeds ranging from striking one's brother to adultery. In contrast, on a beautiful island roofed with azure skies and carpeted with lush meadows, the virtuous spend their days in the joyous activities they had known in this world; poetry, dancing, athletics.

Among the *philosophers* were those who believed that life ends totally and completely with death and those who were convinced that there was an after-life. There was no agreement on what this after-life would be like. One author simply holds out the possibility of eternal happiness and sees this especially as a reward for those who have served their nation with honor and justice.

Graveyards generally provide clear indications of how *ordinary people* react to death. Tombstone inscriptions, the size and kind of monuments, and so on, show the popular attitude to death better than scholarly or poetic writing. Walk through a cemetery and you will be surprised at how much you learn about what the families of those buried there felt when facing death.

Scholars have made a study of many hundreds of tombstones in first-century Rome to get a sense of what the ordinary Roman family believed when it consigned the body of one of its members to the grave. Cemeteries have yielded great numbers of inscriptions like: "Farewell." "Your life is over. Farewell." "No one is immortal." "They have died without having deserved it." "I lift up my hands against the gods who took me away even though I had done no harm."

These samples are enough to show that whatever the poets or philosophers might have taught, there was a strong feeling among average citizens that death was the end of everything.

Christian tombstones stand in stark contrast to these pagan cries of despair. Christians marked their graves with anchors, the symbol of hope; with doves, which represented the soul flying to God; with palm branches, the sign of victory. Inscriptions reveal sentiments like; "May you live in peace and pray for us." "Live in God." "Live in peace." "Live forever."

The Christians had no doubts that life continued with God even after the body had been struck down.

JUDAISM AND DEATH

The attitudes of the Jews passed through a long history of development.

The early Old Testament shows a belief in Sheol, the shadowy world of the dead where survival is such a pale reflection of earthly life that it is not really life at all.

Reflection on the kind of God Yahweh is gradually gave form to a new mood toward death. If Yahweh is the God of life, then death is a denial of his power. As long as death snuffs out life, then God's power is somehow limited. God's conquest of death would seem to be necessary as the sign of his ultimate rule over everything.

Then there is the perennial problem of evil. Human experience shows that injustice in the world is not resolved here. Good people suffer, while the evil often seem to prosper. The evil sometimes torment the good and nothing happens to them because of this.

How can a God who is good, who knows the hearts of men, allow evil, permit injustice?

The answer that emerged was that life continues after death. In that life, all that seemed unfair, unable to be squared with a good and loving God, is made right.

HOW DOES MAN LIVE AFTER DEATH?

Descriptions of the after-life were bewildering in their diversity.

For those in the Greek cultural circle which believed in immortality, the soul was imprisoned in the body. The advantage of the after-life was liberation from the body; to become free, pure, unattached to the burdens of bodilyness. For such people, the idea of a resurrection of the body was nonsense because it meant putting back on what was best gotten rid of. To have a body in the after-life would be like carrying terminal cancer with one forever.

The idea that man might not only live forever but that his body would be part of that life first found expression in the Old Testament in the second century B. C. In the Second Book of Maccabees, seven young brothers are tortured and executed for refusing to give up their faith. Each affirms his belief in eternal life. One brother, putting out his tongue and hands for the torturers, exclaims, "It was from Heaven that I received these; for the sake of his laws I disdain them; from him I hope to receive them again" (2 Mac 7.11).

At the time of Jesus, one group of Jews, the Sadducees, denied the resurrection of the body. Another sect, the Pharisees, believed that since the body and soul form one man, if there was survival for man, it had to be for him as he is, a composite of body and soul. How exactly the resurrected body would be formed and what the next life would be like was fair game for speculation.

Many rabbis envisioned life very much as it is now except that defects would be corrected and unpleasant and difficult situations would be done away with.

WHAT WAS HAPPENING AT CORINTH

Precisely why Paul felt he had to raise the issue of the resurrection of the body with the Corinthians is not clear. We do not have the questions as the delegation brought them to Paul. We can only try to reconstruct what Paul was responding to from what he writes.

One, or both, of two errors was confusing the Corinthians. The first was in line with the Greek philosophy already mentioned. If the body is the prison of the soul, then a resurrection of the body is not at all to be desired. In fact, it is a step backward because it means putting the soul back into the dungeon from which it has escaped.

The other error moves in a different direction. Many early Christians believed that Jesus, who had died and had risen from the dead, would come very soon to bring his rule to the world. They expected that the second coming of Jesus would mark the end of the world as they knew it and its replacement by the world as God intended it to be. As time went on and this glorious event did not occur, some Christians began to look less to the future and to see all of God's promises fulfilled here and now. Thus, resurrection from the dead does not belong to some far-off future but has already happened. Through Baptism, the Christian has died to his old life of sin and has already begun a new life. This is perfectly true, except that when pushed to its farthest limits, such an idea neglects that part of Jesus' teaching and Christian belief that accepts the wonderful character of life now but still looks to total fulfillment in the future. Thus, at one end were some who held that there is no resurrection at all, that the resurrection of the body is a repugnant and ridiculous concept. At the other were some who maintained that the resurrection from the dead is a

spiritual reality that has happened already to such an extent
that there is no special future to await.

Paul instructs the Christians on the meaning of resurrection.

THE TRADITION (3-8)

Using the same technical words he had used when teaching
about the Eucharist, Paul tells the Corinthians that he "handed
on to them what he himself had received." Paul had been
taught about the resurrection very early in his career as a
Christian and he shared that teaching with the Corinthians
when he first preached to them.

These verses are an ancient Christian creed with a few addi-
tions by Paul. The creed makes four basic statements about
Jesus Christ:
he died
he was buried
he rose
he was seen.

CHRIST DIED FOR OUR SINS IN ACCORDANCE
WITH THE SCRIPTURES

A reason is attached to the simple statement that Jesus died
— for our sins. How Paul understood Jesus' death belongs
to another discussion to be taken up in another booklet.

The Scripture that was understood as the foretelling of
Jesus' death was probably a passage from the Servant of
Yahweh poems mentioned previously. The Servant, suffering though guiltless, "surrendered himself to death and was
counted among the wicked; and he shall take away the sins
of many, and win pardon for their sins" (Is 53.12).

HE WAS BURIED

A simple, stark statement. When the door of the tomb was
rolled closed, Jesus was consigned to the land of the dead.

HE ROSE (=WAS RAISED) ON THE THIRD DAY

Jesus either "rose" (in which case the emphasis is on Christ's own power) or "was raised" (in which case the emphasis is on the action of the Father). Either translation of the Greek is possible. Whichever is adopted does not make much difference as far as meaning goes. The "was raised" version in no way belittles the power of Jesus himself.

Jesus' resurrection involved moving from one kind of existence to another. Jesus' resurrection from the dead was not like the situation of Lazarus in the Gospel story. Lazarus was called back to life, but to the same life he had lived before. He escaped death once, but only for a while since sometime in the future it would claim him again. Jesus passed into an existence so filled with the life of God that he was free forever of the power of death.

For Paul, Jesus' body is part of the whole person that entered this new kind of existence. Jesus' resurrected body is transformed to reveal his divinity fully and clearly.

Paul avoids overly physical descriptions which would make the body a fancier version of what it is here. In verses 35 and following, Paul makes it clear that the bodily part of human existence continues in the the world of the resurrection but there is a great difference between the body as it is now and the body as it will be then. We will return to this shortly in considering the resurrection of the body.

HE WAS SEEN

There is some discussion about which is the better translation of the Greek word used here, "he was seen" or "he appeared."

Many scholars would hold that "appeared" is more in tune with the way the word is ordinarily used. The emphasis is not so much on the one who has the experience of "seeing" but on God or Jesus who "makes himself seen."

What was involved in the experience of an appearance of Jesus to Cephas, the Twelve, the five hundred brothers, James, the apostles, Paul?

Remember we are dealing with realities that are very hard to talk about. Putting experiences of God into human words is an almost impossible task. How does one "see" the invisible, the spiritual God? How does one "see" the resurrected Jesus? Obviously, "seeing" God, "seeing" Jesus Christ risen from the dead is not the same as seeing a tree, or seeing John Smith. God, or here the Risen Jesus Christ, makes his presence felt.

This does not mean that what takes place comes from inside the one who has the experience. Suppose someone works on my suggestibility and describes in vivid detail the progress of a large spider crawling up my back. I begin to squirm to reach the spider. I even feel a slight tickle where I believe the spider to be inching along. But it turns out to be a practical joke. There was no spider on my back, only in the inventive ability of my mind helped by the power of suggestion.

This is not the case of an appearance. Though an appearance of the Lord could never be proved scientifically, the emphasis is on the fact that the recipient does not invent or imagine the experience. In a mysterious way, beyond ordinary seeing and hearing, the Lord truly communicated with the privileged person. Jesus Christ reached into a human life and we can only use the words of common experience, like "seeing," to describe this remarkable event.

Paul's conduct before and after the Lord appeared to him is an indication that he was not super-imaginative or hallucinating. As he himself related, Saul, the pious and dedicated Jew, hunting down Christians with a towering sense of the rightness of what he was doing, turned drastically and became not only a Christian but a fervent missionary.

PAUL'S PURPOSE IN QUOTING THE CREED

Paul was not interested in trying to prove Jesus' resurrection. In recalling to the Corinthians this familiar creed about the death, burial, resurrection and appearances of Jesus, Paul was simply reminding them of something already part of their faith. He moves from the resurrection of Jesus to resurrection for all.

CHRIST AS THE "FIRST FRUITS" (20-28)

The laws of the Hebrew Bible stipulated that a portion of the first ripe grain gathered in the harvest be offered to God. This ceremony confessed God as the source of the whole crop. All the produce of the golden fields belongs to the Lord of nature, the Lord of all creation, Yahweh. In offering a small portion, the Israelite farmer symbolized the offering of the whole crop.

Once God had been recognized as the source and rightful owner of the crop, the farmer was free to use it for his own purposes.

Note that by offering a sample, the "first-fruits," the farmer really caused the rest of his crop to be offered also.

Jesus Christ was the "first-fruits" of humanity. He was the first to reach full maturity, to come to term, to enter the life of fullness with God. His moving into that new life affected not only him but caused all men to be capable of entering the same life.

Because Jesus rose, resurrection from the dead becomes possible for all. But this has to happen according to God's plan. All those who belong to him will in time rise from the dead. This resurrection will signal the ultimate victory of God. Death, the sum total of all that stands against the Living God (sickness, weakness, sin, evil), is most obvious in physical death. The absolute and final sign that God has conquered total death will be the breaking of the

94

chains of physical death. The resurrection will be life bursting through where death seemed to be king.

THE BODY AFTER RESURRECTION (35-49)

Paul plunges bravely ahead to try to answer some difficult questions.

"How are the dead to be raised up? " "What kind of body will they have? "

Paul is much more careful and sober in his reply than later generations of theologians, preachers and teachers would be.

Paul begins with two examples from common experience. There is the seed of grain which is planted, dies, and is the source of a new living plant. There is the staggering variety of bodies among created things: the bodies of men, of animals, of birds, of fish, of the sun, the stars, the moon.

These examples stress the power of God as creator. If God is able to create this wonderful diversity of bodies, then it should not be difficult to believe that he can also create a body to suit living with him forever.

After setting the stage, Paul gets to the heart of his explanation. He speaks of the "natural body" and the "spiritual body." By body, Paul means the human person in his entirety; his personality, his characteristics, his relationships with others.

The natural body is man's total self now. It is *subject to decay*. There is a slow process of dying on every level. Physically each moment is one step closer to the grave. Talents and abilities flower and then begin to wither. Man's life now is *ignoble* because vulnerable to the erosion of the proper, peace-begetting relationships that ought to exist between man and God and man and man. Man's total life now is characterized by *weakness*, by the distance that stretches between himself and God, the source of life and strength.

The spiritual body is man's total person as it will be when flooded totally by the life of the Spirit. Then, that person will be *incorruptible*. Any form of death that could taint the vigor and fullness of life is eliminated. The resurrected person will be *glorious*. Glory is a way of talking about a reflection, a manifestation of God. All aspects of the life of the resurrected person will mirror God's beautiful and perfect life. Life for the spiritual body will be *strength*, because the resurrected person will be living in unbreakable union with God, the source of strength.

There will be a continuity between man as he is now, man as soul and body, man as involved with others, and man in the life after death. At the same time, man will experience a deep and real transformation because the total self that he is, soul and body, will be filled with the life of God himself.

THE RESURRECTION TODAY

1. For Paul and Christians, the cross and resurrection belong together. The cross finds its completion in the resurrection.

2. There is a future after death, a future in which men and women will be taken into the life of God himself.

3. Each person will live this future as a total human being, a being of body and soul, as he is in this life.

4. Jesus Christ, by his resurrection from the dead, has already entered into that life with God. In his resurrection, his body was transformed to become the kind of body suitable to being united to divinity.

5. Jesus Christ entered that life as the leader for all men. Through his death and resurrection, Jesus blazed a trail for all men to follow.

6. Words fail in trying to describe what life with God, the

life of the resurrection will be. Paul speaks in terms of each of us being the same as he is here. We shall be the same persons we are now. At the same time, we shall be different. We shall be humans whose whole reality reflects closeness to God. There will be no room for imperfection, for unhappiness, for anything which would cloud the life of God we shall carry within ourselves.

SUGGESTIONS FOR REFLECTION

1. As you think back over your lifetime experiences with death, what are your feelings toward it? Have you continued on as though the deceased one(s) were living or gone forever? What kind of God does your attitude presume?

2. The ancient Christian creed quoted by Paul makes four basic statements about Jesus Christ: he died, he was buried, he rose, he was seen. Since the Apostles' Creed and the Nicene Creed that we use today say much more, what does this tell us about the nature and development of Creeds?

3. Try to explain the meaning of "Jesus rose from the dead" to one other person.

4. Do you generally tend to think of bodies as good or as bad? What are a few things you do that show you regard the body as good? What are a few things that show you regard it as bad? What do you mean by "body"? Is yours the same meaning as Paul's?

5. Try to put into words what you mean by "life." Next, try to put into words what you mean by "Life in God." Then try to put into words what you mean by "heaven." Use analogies from your own experience of "Life-filled," or list a few adjectives that would express this condition. How does your idea compare with Paul's?

CHAPTER VIII

AT THE END

We have reached the end of this part of our efforts to understand the lasting truth that Paul has to offer regarding many of the most significant issues of life.

We have read and reflected on Paul's letter to a community of Christians he founded. Knowing our own clumsy and fumbling attempts at understanding and living the way of Jesus, we should be willing to accept the Corinthians as our brothers and sisters, in whom we find the same mixture of good and bad, of nobility and cheapness that clashes in ourselves.

The Corinthians desire to follow Christ, who taught and brought unity, yet they are separated by misunderstanding over how one comes to know Christ better.

The Corinthians desire to serve God, but their shabby squabbles over recognition undo his work.

The Corinthians boast of their freedom but become enslaved to selfishness.

The Corinthians celebrate the Lord's Supper, but shame their participation but neglecting the needs of their brothers and sisters.

The Corinthians rejoice in the future Jesus has won for them, but go astray in attempts to understand it better.

Each of us could probably subsistute "I" for "the Corinthians" in the above statements without too much stretching of the truth.

Paul, pastor and theologian, shows the way to them and to us. He enlightens them and us about true wisdom, about the Church, about the different roles different people play in the Church, about real freedom, about the implications of the Eucharist, about the resurrection.

What remains is for us is to take Paul's principles and apply them to our situation today. What remains for us is to be a community open to the Spirit and not millions of individuals each going his own way. What remains for us is to have the courage to face the truth. What remains for us is to follow the way of Jesus as taught by Paul.

What remains for us is to be the presence of Jesus Christ in this terrible and wonderful twentieth century world.

SUGGESTIONS FOR REFLECTION

1. After trying to answer some of these questions yourself, and to put answers into words, how do you think Paul came to the insights he expressed about wisdom, the Church, roles in the Church, freedom, the Eucharist, and the resurrection in this letter? Do you find his explanations clear for you and your life? What can you do to make them more a part of your life?

2. Take each of the times the word "Corinthians" occurs in this post-script, insert instead the name of your parish and town. Then re-read it with the inserts to get a better idea of the universality of the human condition and the message for all communities in the Body of Christ.